WILDFLOWERS
for
ALL SEASONS

Other Books by Ghillean T. Prance

AMAZONIA (with T. E. Lovejoy)

ÁRVORES DE MANAUS

LEAVES

WILDFLOWERS
for
ALL SEASONS

Paintings by Anna Vojtech

Text by Ghillean T. Prance

CROWN PUBLISHERS, INC., NEW YORK

Published by Crown Publishers, Inc., 225 Park Avenue South,
New York, New York 10003.
CROWN is a trademark of Crown Publishers, Inc.
Manufactured in Japan
Book design by Dana Sloan

Library of Congress Cataloging-in-Publication Data

Prance, Ghillean T., 1937–
Wildflowers for all seasons/paintings by Anna Vojtech; text
by Ghillean T. Prance.
1. Wild flowers—New England—Pictorial works. 2. Wild
flowers—New England—Identification. 3. Botanical
illustration—New England. 4. Flower painting and
illustration—New England. I. Vojtech, Anna. II. Title.
QK121.P73 1989
582.13′0974—dc19
ISBN 0-517-57007-6

10 9 8 7 6 5 4 3 2 1
First Edition

Contents

Preface

by ANNA VOJTECH

Since I was a little girl, I have always liked collecting herbs and flowers. I dried them and then wanted to make magic with them. My dream, inspired by fairy tales, was to become an herb witch. My most memorable ambition was to conjure up a little doll with blinking eyes.

I was fascinated by the beauty of flowers. I tried to paint them in my sketch book. But I was never satisfied with the result of my artwork in comparison with nature's.

Later, when I was able to travel throughout Europe with my friends, I would get a yearning to be back home again and walk through the forests and over the melancholic Czech countryside. The aroma of those flowers is like nowhere else in the world. They are the sweet fragrance of my homeland, Czechoslovakia.

The reality of life caught up with my romantic youth. It sometimes happens that political events influence and change our lives. So one day I appeared upon the American continent. At one time I never would have believed that the stream of life would carry me all the way to Canada and then to New England.

I found myself in a new and strange world, very different from all the romantic imaginings of my countrymen. My American husband and I first lived in Montreal. Even if Montreal is a pleasant city, it couldn't replace my Prague. I asked myself if I would ever fit into this new environment. How should I let my roots grow into another soil?

Then our son Mathis was born. And suddenly I began to feel a great desire for the smell of fresh air and clean earth. I remembered the country as a great source of my childhood happiness, and so we decided to leave the city.

For six beautiful years we lived in the hill country of the Eastern Townships not far from the Vermont border. It was here I began painting wildflowers again. And here our second son, Lukas, was born.

For most of the models for my paintings I didn't have to go far. Our colorful meadow was surrounded by a forest full of spring flowers. I always looked for flowers, even when driving my car. I had to force my eyes to follow a curve in the road instead of letting them wander along the roadsides. I knew the flowers in the ditches better than the traffic signs. Yellow Canada lily that I couldn't find nearby grew in profusion three and a half miles east. If one of us had a cough, I'd drive three miles west to pick coltsfoot leaves. When Mathis was still a baby we would take long excursions into the countryside and return with the baby carriage loaded down with herbs, looking like a camouflaged battlewagon.

The people in our area knew about my preoccupation at times with collecting and painting wildflowers. Through this work I found many new friends. Some people brought me flowers and told me where to find others. The flowers in my collection are interwoven with all kinds of people, exciting situations, and adventurous stories.

My trophies were kept in the refrigerator; there they did not wilt in hot weather. Some flowers are impossible to keep alive for more than a few hours. The orange hawk-weed is extremely sensitive. It took ten plants to complete a painting that reflects, and then only inadequately, some of its fresh liveliness. The touch-me-not reacts true to its name. I attempted many times to take one home, but each time it died before I arrived.

Some flowers bloom only part of the day. The chicory blooms from morning till noon. Evening primrose opens its blossoms in the afternoon.

I dug up most of the flowers I painted with their roots well attached, and when finished with them I replanted them around the house. But only a few of them managed to make it the next year. I have recognized how alive and free-spirited wildflowers really are. They will choose their soil and environment themselves.

Throughout the years I have managed to put together a collection of paintings showing a cross section of wildflowers that appear season by season in the northeastern United States and Canada. It begins with the first flower in spring and ends with the last in autumn. Yet winter, too, has its own profusion of intricate patterns and shapes. Paintings of dried flowers are also part of this collection.

We now live in Marblehead, Massachusetts, a small seaside town north of Boston. To my surprise I haven't stopped working on my collection. I still find many fascinating flowers, many of which do not grow in the northern part of New England. I also travel to Connecticut and western Massachusetts to find flowers that don't grow along the coast or in the north.

My paintings have been exhibited in many places. In this way I share my flowers with others. It gives me a great deal of satisfaction.

But a collection of paintings is not yet a book. Finding the right text was a problem. Who would write it and how should it be written? Where would I find a person who would not only have the knowledge but also the feeling, imagination, and style that would complement my paintings?

It was the friendly hand of fate that led me to Bertha Klausner, not only a wonderful literary agent, but a warm friend and an intuitive woman, who brought me together with Dr. Ghillean Prance. With his highly knowledgeable and sensitive text, part of my collection could finally become this book.

My special thanks to my husband Roland Baumgaertel for his patience and understanding; my sons Mathis and Lukas for their lively presence; all my friends for their support; neighbors and friends from the Eastern Townships in Canada for their priceless advice and direction; and Monsieur Pierre Bourgue, Director of the Botanical Garden in Montreal, who was the first one to exhibit my collection of wildflowers. Many thanks also to Dr. Peter Ashton, Director of the Arnold Arboretum of Harvard University, who introduced me to Lincoln Foster and his wife, Timmy, whose knowledge and friendship were to me the greatest support of all.

Introduction

by GHILLEAN T. PRANCE

I have known for a long time of the beautiful flower paintings of Anna Vojtech and was surprised when she came to my office with the offer to write a text to accompany a selection of her work on the New England flora. Although I was too busy to accept such an offer, no one could turn down the opportunity to work with such attractive and botanically accurate illustrations. Our day of anguish came in a hotel room in New York City when we had to select only one hundred twenty-nine of the over three hundred paintings that were available. As we put some beautiful paintings into the reject pile, I could see the artist's face become more dejected as some of her treasures and friends that she herself has written about so ably in her preface were cast aside. After much anguish we came up with the selection of her paintings that is presented here as representative of the four seasons of the year.

You will note in the descriptions that many of the plants we have chosen originated in Europe. They are now fully naturalized and common wildflowers of the New England area, but they are plants that were either brought over by the colonists for their many uses—as medicines, vegetables, or ornamentals, for instance—or they are accidental introductions that hitched a ride in grain seed, in packing cases, or in some other way. Perhaps the number of introduced plants that make up our final selection reflects the European origin of both authors. We have managed to include some of the plants with which we grew up, that influenced our early years and led to our love of nature. Both the artist and myself became fascinated with flowers at an early age and were deeply influenced in our career choices by the time spent in the woods and meadows of Europe among the wildflowers.

We have also included many native American plants that do not occur in Europe or are only there as introductions. The number of native plants is apparent by the numerous descriptions that mention ways in which Native Americans used the plants. These great people used most of the plants around them in some way or another, especially as foods or medicines. Many medicinal uses of the plants are mentioned in the text, but this should not be taken as a prescription on how to use these plants. Medicinal plants are generally poisonous plants taken in small doses and therefore should not be used without extensive knowledge. It takes years of training and apprenticeship to become an Indian healer, so this book is not a guide for self-treatment. Nevertheless, it is significant that fifty percent of the prescription drugs that we use today were originally derived from plants and that about twenty-five percent are still extracted from plants. Many of these drugs have been learned about from the rich folklore of indigenous peoples around the world who have lived close to the plants that surrounded them.

Another word of caution! The plants that are illustrated here are beautiful. Some have been introduced into the gardens of the world and are already well-known. It is tempting to gather up bulbs and roots of dutchman's breeches, lady's slipper orchids, or wild yellow lilies, but this should not be done because it is one of the causes of the rarity and endangerment of so many of our wildflowers. For gardens, plants should be obtained from a nursery where the propagules have come from cultivated sources and not from the wild. We must leave the native species to continue their existence for future generations. We are surrounded by many beautiful flowers—go out and enjoy them in the fields and woodlands. We hope, too, that during the cold of winter you can enjoy them through the paintings here.

This is a book of seasons that shows the gradual progression of flowering throughout the year. The texts begin with the most-used common name. But, as the long list of additional names under many species indicates, the common name is not always a reliable guide to the exact identity of a plant. The scientific Latin name, which is unique to each species, is also given. According to international convention this is followed by the abbreviated form of the name of the author who described the species, for example with an *L.* for Linnaeus. Since many of the plants treated here are common members of the European flora, a large number were described by Linnaeus, the founder of modern botanical nomenclature. Each plant has two Latin names, the first representing the genus and the second the species to which it belongs. Each genus of plants belongs to a higher group. The family and the plant family names are also given. This identifying information is followed by a text that does not try to give a full botanical description, for that can be found in any field guide on flora. Instead some of the most interesting facts about each species are given, as well as a summary of their natural distribution range. Inevitably some technical botanical terms are used, and these are defined in a glossary at the end of the text.

The writing of these descriptions would not have been possible without the help of David Johnson and the library of The New York Botanical Garden. I am extremely grateful to my wife, Anne E. Prance, for her careful review of the text, and to Rosemary Lawlor for typing and word processing the several draft versions of the manuscript.

SPRING

Out of the shadow of exhausting, interminable winter come the first signs of awakening life.

The air is filled with the coming of spring.

I cannot trust the weather yet and strain to watch the clouds, hoping there will be no more snow this year. The unrelenting grip of the cold has worn us out, and we long for spring and renewal. Sometimes the clouds are merciless; but even so my Canadian diary reads . . .

March 26. Today I found a few shoots of marsh marigold in a ditch by the road. Some reeds have sprouted near the pond, which is still covered with ice. Nearby in a shallow pool of water I saw a swarm of tadpoles darting about. A butterfly flashed around my head, the first one to be lured out by the warm sun. In the dried-out grass of last year, metallic blue beetles rustle about and the sallows are covered with the velvety blooms that give them the name *pussy willow.*

March 28. The colors are changing. The hills are tinged with pink and lilac taint, the maple buds are opening, suffusing the mountainsides with rose. Willows glisten in fresh yellow. The earth, no longer burdened with a heavy blanket of snow, breathes easily again and exhales a hundred perfumes of spring.

We feel no regret when we bid winter good-bye. We embrace new life.

April 5. In the gardens of people's houses, I saw the first snowdrops and crocuses; soon daffodils will come. Wild nature wisely awakens more slowly and cautiously than the carefully tended gardens. There is no human hand to ward off the last clasp of cold. Bulbs, roots, and seeds, which in a little while will send up shoots to the sun, are buried deep in the soil beyond the reach of frost.

· *April 10.* The shadows of the sheltered woods still hold patches of wet snow, but there are also the twin leaves of trout lilies standing green above gray forest ground. . . . Startling ribbon-green pyramids, the first sight of the false hellebore, fight their way through last year's mat of leaves. In the swamps frogs are rehearsing for a spring performance.

April 20. In the shade of a big maple tree I found a fragile, dazzling white flower with a bright yellow center. It is bloodroot. Its single leaf is curled and wrapped around each stalk like a protective, ancient scroll. How curious, I think, and wonder what its message might be. . . .

Nothing can hold the flow of new life now. Amazing things are happening overnight. Suddenly the ditches, swamps, and stream banks are covered with golden nuggets of marsh marigolds. The meadow in the front of our house lives through amazing metamorphoses: a soft yellow blanket of dandelions soon changes into a white carpet of blossoming wild strawberries. And an invisible, mysterious hand weaves new color into this masterpiece almost every day.

Nature doesn't wait for me. Take what is here right now, tomorrow it might not be there anymore!

Somebody just called about a place where I might find yellow lady's slipper. I have been searching for four years. Hurry up, Anna, fight your way through the swarms of blackflies, find the flower *now,* and paint and paint!

Anna Vojtech

Skunk Cabbage

Symplocarpus foetidus (L. Nutt.)

Family: *Araceae*
Arum family

Additional names:
bear weed, foetid hellebore, meadow cabbage, polecat weed, skunk weed

In spite of the fact that this plant smells strongly, as both its common and scientific names imply, it is a welcome harbinger of spring and its earliest-flowering plant. Skunk cabbage's ability to flower while snow is still around it comes, in part, from a characteristic it shares with many aroids: it produces heat. The temperature increase, which helps to melt the snow, is from the chemical reaction that produces the flower's scent to attract insect pollinators. But the oniony smell that gives the plant its names comes from the sap.

The skunk cabbage is found in swampy places and bogs, beside streams in the northeastern and central United States, and also in eastern Asia.

The cultivated arum and calla lilies and the wild jack-in-the-pulpit are members of the same plant family, Araceae. This family has a characteristic and easily recognized flower with a large flower leaf or spathe enveloping a compact inflorescence called a spadix.

The seeds and roots are used in folk medicine and in herbal ointments and powders to treat many ailments such as rheumatic pains, catarrh, and convulsions. The Micmac Indians crushed the leaves and inhaled the vapor as a headache remedy. Various tribes of American Indians have cooked and eaten the young leaves like spinach. The unpleasant smell and taste were removed by changing the water two or three times during the boiling process. It has also been noted that bears like to eat the skunk-cabbage roots.

Bloodroot

Sanguinaria canadensis L.

Family: *Papaveraceae Poppy family*

Additional names:
coon root, paucon, pauson, puccoon root, red Indian paint, redroot, snake-bite, sweet slumber, tatterwort

Like many other early spring flowers such as the trout lily, the bloodroot has large underground modified stems or rhizomes in which it stores nutrients to survive the winter and that allow it to leaf and flower quickly as soon as the winter recedes. The nutrients, husbanded from the previous year, produce a single palmate leaf and only one flower, although occasionally two flowers are found on one stem. The flowers are white and sometimes tinged with pink or purple.

The common name *bloodroot* and the Latin name *Sanguinaria* are used because, like many plants in the poppy family, the root has a profuse, orange milky latex or sap. If the root is broken, this sap oozes out like blood.

One of its common names, *sweet slumber,* points to its effectiveness as a calmative in traditional medicine. Analysis has found it to have various chemically active compounds, including the alkaloid protopine, which is also found in opium, another member of the poppy family. Protopine is now known to depress heart action and cause nausea and vomiting. However, if it is used in small doses it can increase the appetite and improve digestion.

Over the years bloodroot has been used to make emetics, cathartics, and expectorants. In 1830 botanist A. Rafinesque said of the bloodroot, "It is one of the most valuable medical articles of our country, and already begins to be introduced into general practice." The root contains another alkaloid, sanguinarine, that is bactericidal. Sanguinarine has recently been found to be useful for the treatment of dental plaque. It is an ingredient in Viadent mouthwash, which has been shown to be effective in lowering plaque counts.

This species is offered for sale in many nursery catalogs. Not all are from propagated plants. If you purchase bloodroot for your garden, be sure that it is not from a wild-collected plant. You certainly will not want to contribute to the depletion of this important member of our flora.

Yellow Trout Lily

Erythronium americanum Ker.

Family: *Liliaceae Lily family*

Additional names:
Eastern trout lily, dogtooth violet

Early in spring, the decaying leaves of autumn are pushed aside as the mottled leaves of the yellow trout lily edge out into the light. They open and lie flat on the dead brown detritus of the eastern woodlands, each leaf a full green with gray-brown piscine mottlings; each almost a promise of fish lurking in the nearby stream shallows. The trout lily, neither a fish nor a true lily, though reminiscent of both, is ready to flower again. It puts up a single flowering stem, or scape, and soon an ephemeral, bell-shaped flower nods its yellow head. At sunset the petals close and are blanketed with purple sepals for the night.

The name *dogtooth violet* came from the European species *(Erythronium dens-canis),* which has purple flowers and corms that resemble the incisor tooth of a dog. It is this tooth-shaped corm that carries the life of a trout lily from year to year, for it stores food during the winter.

Such a ready larder can be disadvantageous to the plant, for it provides food for hungry animals during the cold winter months. The trout lily's form of protection is a self-burying strategy. After flowering the leaves die, the flower stalk wilts, and as a consequence the developing fruit capsule is dropped to the forest floor where it remains until the seeds are ripe. They germinate near the surface and form a small corm in their first year. The following year the corm sends down runners to form another corm a few inches deeper. This process occurs for about five years, gradually burying the corm deeper until the corm of the mature trout lily is about fifteen inches under the forest floor.

Purple Trillium

**Trillium erectum
L.**

Family: *Liliaceae
Lily family*

Additional names:
*bethroot, bethworth,
birthroot, brown Beth, ill-
scented trillium, Indian
balm, much hunger, nose
bleed, red Benjamin, red
trillium, squawroot,
stinking Benjamin,
stinkin' Willie, wake-
robin, wet-dog trillium*

Trilliums are probably the best known of the native North American wildflowers. Here, in the wild, they signal spring's arrival, and elsewhere they are popular as cultivated plants. The name *trillium* is derived from the Latin word *tres,* meaning three, because of the whorl of three leaves that are borne below the single deep purple-red flower. The flowers are occasionally white, and the plant can thus be confused with the large-flowered trillium *(T. grandiflorum).* However, purple trillium differs in its smaller flowers with narrower petals and a black center.

The purple trillium is an eastern species that is found from Ontario and the Gaspé Peninsula to the mountains of Georgia. Farther west it is replaced by other species, such as *Trillium flexipes.* The purple trillium grows over a wide range of habitats and soil types. It can be found in springtime in moraines, shallow soils, talus slopes, open woods, and sandy areas. The species name *erectum* refers to the erect flower stalk, which contrasts to the reflexed stalk of various other species.

This plant must have more common names than most other North American species. Many different species of plants are often called by these same names, a fact that emphasizes the usefulness of the Latin names, which are applied uniformly to a species throughout its range.

Some of the common names are descriptive of the plant, such as those referring to the flower's color or the smell of the plant. This trillium is commonly regarded as having a strong smell, rather like that of a wet dog.

Other common names derive from uses to which this plant has been put. Because the roots can be rubbed to produce a soapy lather it has been called *bath root,* and because the young leaves were eaten as a survival food it is sometimes called *much hunger.*

Indian and folk medicine usages have given rise to many other names. The roots were used to make a poultice to relieve bee stings, hence the name *bee root.* The rhizomes of various trillium species have been used as astringents, pectorals, tonics, and expectorants. Purple trillium's name *squawroot* reflects its use by Indians for treatment of gynecological disorders and to aid in childbirth.

Modern chemical analysis has shown that the roots of purple trillium contain minute quantities of interesting steroid compounds: bethogenin, diosgenin, pennogenin, and fecogenin—compounds similar to those used today in birth-control pills.

Blue Marsh Violet

Viola cucullata
Ait.

Family: *Violaceae*
Violet family

I know a bank where the wild thyme blows,
Where oxslips and the nodding violet grows
Quite over-canopied with luscious wood-bine,
With sweet musk roses, and with eglantine.
A Midsummer Night's Dream, *II.i.254–257*

I think the king is but a man, as I am.
The violet smells to him as it doth to me.
Henry V, *IV.i.101–102*

A violet in the youth of primy nature,
Forward, not permanent, sweet, not lasting.
The perfume and suppliance of a minute,
No more.
Hamlet, *I.iii.7–9*

Shakespeare combined his insight into the human heart and his ability to observe details about the natural world. These quotations tell us much of both, as he reveals the innate longing for the sensuous experience, the commonality of king and subject, the haunting transience of life and the sadness of loss. Each of these is revealed by the symbol of the nodding, fragrant, early blooming, transient violet.

The blue marsh violet is one species of a large genus of plants with a wide distribution in the cooler parts of the world. This species is found over a large area, north to Quebec and Ontario, south to Georgia, west to Arkansas, and east to New England. It grows in bogs and other wet places at all elevations. The pale violet flowers open in April, May, or June. Sometimes the petals are pure white, but they are veined with violet, and all the flowers have a dark eye zone at their center to attract the insects that will pollinate them.

Bluets

Houstonia
caerulea
L.

Family: *Rubiaceae*
Madder family

Additional name:
angel eyes

This charming small plant occurs in the open woods and grasslands of the northeastern United States and adjacent Canada. It grows easily and often invades fields in areas with acid soils. It is an early spring flower that varies in color from lavender to whitish, becoming yellow with age. It is not truly blue as the name would infer.

These tiny plants have small opposite leaves and flowers with the parts in fours. The flowers are interesting because they occur in two forms. Some plants have flowers with protruding pollen-bearing stamens and a short style, while others have included stamens and a long style. This phenomenon—known as heterostyly—occurs in a number of plant families including the madder and the primrose families. The pollen from a long-styled plant must reach a short-styled one to fertilize the ovule successfully. This is a mechanism that has evolved to ensure cross-pollination and thus avoid inbreeding.

Bluets are readily cultivated in a wildflower garden on acid soil, where they make a welcome addition to the early spring flowers. In the central United States bluets are replaced by summer bluets *(H. ciliolata),* an excellent rock garden plant.

Coltsfoot

Tussilago fafara
L.

Family: *Asteraceae*
Aster family

Additional names:
*ass's foot, clayweed,
coughwort, donnhove,
fieldhove, foalswort,
horsehoof*

*A thousand years will come and go,
And thousands more will rise,
My buried bones to dust will grow
And dust defile my eyes,
But when the lark sings o'er the world
And the swallow weaves her nest,
My soul will take the coltsfoot gold
And blossom on my breast.*

Alfred Williams

This early spring flower with small, dandelionlike flowers is a native of Europe. It was such a popular flower that it was quickly introduced to North America, where it is now common on roadsides and waste ground throughout New England and beyond. The attractive yellow flowers push through thick clay on roadsides and other waste places, giving rise to another local name, *clayweed.* It is a popular plant because it brightens those barren areas immediately after winter is over.

The Latin name of this plant is informative. *Tussilago,* the generic name created by Linnaeus, refers to the plant's medicinal properties. It comes from *tussis ago,* meaning to drive out a cough. The species name *fafara* comes from the word *fafarus,* the old name for white poplar, because of a resemblance between the leaves.

The Romans called coltsfoot *filius ante patrem,* or son before father, referring to the fact that the flowers emerge and die down before the leaves are produced. People sometimes fail to link the leaves with the flowers of this plant because they are produced at different times.

However, its name is derived from the leaves. The most-used common name for this plant, *coltsfoot,* and the many other names referring to the hooves of domestic animals arose from the shape of the leaf, which is reminiscent of the hoofprint of a horse. The young leaves are covered by a woolly fuzz that falls off as the leaves mature. This fuzz was used as a material for fire starting in ancient times.

Like the dandelion, coltsfoot produces seeds with a parachute of silky hairs, or pappus, to carry them on the breeze and disperse them widely. This mass of soft down is used by goldfinches to line their nests and was widely used by the Highlanders of Scotland to stuff pillows and mattresses.

Coltsfoot is one of the earliest known herbal medicines and was extolled by Dioscorides and Pliny and many later herbalists, a fact obviously known by Linnaeus when he named the genus. The herbals of Gerard and Culpeper tell about its medicinal uses, mainly as a remedy for coughs. It has been used as a decoction to drink and as a source of smoke to inhale. However, caution should be used because scientists in Japan recently discovered that dried flowers of coltsfoot caused cancerous tumors in rats.

Wild Ginger

Asarum canadense L.

Family: *Aristolochiaceae Birthwort family*

Additional names: *asarabacca, Canada snakeroot, colic root, false coltsfoot, Indian ginger*

Chippewa and Ojibwe Indians ate wild gingerroot. They used it as an appetizer and also to flavor many of their cooked foods. It is aromatic and gives food an agreeable but slightly acid taste.

As is often the case, many folk uses of this plant are well founded on fact. Wild ginger has been used as a stimulant, carminative, diuretic, and diaphoretic. It is held to be very effective for stomach ailments. Modern research has found it to contain aristolochic acid, which has proven antimicrobial action against a broad spectrum of bacteria and fungi. It has a volatile oil that has been used in the perfume industry. It also contains a resin and a bitter substance called asaron.

Wild ginger is a small, creeping aromatic herb that sends up paired leaves from the branch tips of its fleshy underground stem. The large, roundish, and velvety leaves have a heart-shaped base, and the solitary bell-shaped flowers are produced in the fork between the leafstalks in April or May. It is a common woodland plant ranging from New Brunswick to North Carolina and west to Kansas and Tennessee.

Although this much-used plant is common and not of striking beauty, its pollination mechanism, called protogyny, is one of precision and fine timing. When the flowers first open, the stigmas are ripe and ready to receive pollen from a visiting fly, but the pollen-bearing stamens are bent away to the side. Only later do they straighten up to the center and shed their pollen. By this method the stigmas are ready before the pollen is shed, so the flowers stand a better chance of cross-pollination by pollen from the flowers of a different plant.

Spring Beauty

Claytonia virginica L.

Family: *Portulacaceae Purslane family*

Spring beauty is common throughout the eastern half of the United States and adjacent Canada. It grows in moist, open woods and grassy thickets, thriving on a wide range of soil types. Its tuber is buried deep underground for warmth during the winter. In spring, a pair of long, narrow, fleshy leaves emerges. They clasp the flower stem, which has many flower buds. The flower stem produces one new flower each day over a two- or three-week period. Each flower has five petals, white or pale pink, each traced with lines of rose.

Linnaeus gave this flower its Latin generic name. He named it in honor of an American botanist, John Clayton, with whom he corresponded. Clayton published *Flora of Virginia* in 1743.

The spring beauty has been the subject of much research by botanists who study plant chromosomes, which carry the genes, or units of inheritance, of any organism. This plant is unusual because the number of chromosomes it carries varies greatly, in contrast to most organisms where the number is constant.

The northern broadleaf spring beauty, *Claytonia caroliniana,* which has a range similar to the spring beauty, is a close relative. It has broader leaves, few flowers, and appears earlier in spring. The spring beauties belong to the purslane family, a family that is characterized by plants with fleshy leaves.

Marsh Marigold

Caltha palustris L.

Family: *Ranunculaceae Buttercup family*

Additional names: *American cowslip, gools, horse blobs, king cups, may blobs, meadow routs, verrucaria, water blobs*

The brilliant gold cup-shaped flowers of the marsh marigolds must have been in Linnaeus's mind when he named the plant *Caltha palustris* (from the Greek word *calathos,* meaning cup, and the Latin *palustris,* meaning of the marsh). Their glossy, gold flowers contrast vibrantly with their shiny, dark green leaves and the ink colors of the sedges and marsh plants around them.

Marsh marigold's many names have arisen because the plant is widespread. It occurs in the northern latitudes in Britain, throughout Europe and into Siberia, as well as in North America.

In the Middle Ages in Europe, May was the month of the Virgin Mary, and the churches held festivals at which wildflowers were used for decoration and offerings. The prolific marsh marigold growing by the streams and in full flower was a perfect choice, and so it gained its name "Mary-gold."

Although one of the brightest of all spring flowers, it lacks petals and instead has five yellow, petallike sepals to attract its insect pollinators to one of their first spring feeds.

The bright flowers have often been used to make dye in England and Scandinavia. The yellow floral pigment can be easily removed from the cell sap of the sepals by boiling them with alum. This gives a rich and delicate dye, which has been used for tinting paper and also for fine silk and cotton. However the color is not permanent, and consequently it is not used widely as a dye.

The medicinal uses of this plant include the use of the sap for curing warts, hence the local name *verrucaria.* However the plant contains protoanemonin, the same irritant oil that buttercups contain, and this can cause rashes.

This plant has been put to several other good uses. The leaves are used as a spinach but must be boiled and the water changed twice to remove the poison they contain. The flower buds are used as a substitute for capers and can have the acrid taste of that condiment. Again the fluid in which the buds are pickled must be removed since it contains poisonous substances.

I don't think it is necessary for me to express my inner feelings in my paintings. Art, like nature, has its own soul. And it is the depth of this soul that I wish to learn more about.

Wood Anemone

Anemone quinquefolia L.

Family: *Ranunculaceae*
Buttercup family

Additional name:
wind flower

A small patch of snow seems to persist in spite of the warm spring days. It stretches out over the blackening leaves of last year's foliage, sodden on the woodland floor. But as the breeze stirs, the snow patch quivers, revealing itself to be not snow, but hundreds of tiny wind flower blossoms, sensitive to the movement of the air. Spring has returned.

Each year these white, starlike flowers return in the woodlands and clearings of the northeast, from Quebec to North Carolina.

Each plant is like a miniature floral arrangement with three or five stalked and deeply divided leaves surrounding the solitary long-stalked white flower. The white "petals" of the flowers are actually sepals, which look like petals, but this species' flowers have no petals. The sepals are often tinted pink to red on the outside. The fruits are hairy and are borne in a globose, furry cluster.

The leaves and roots of anemones contain protoanemonin, an irritant that can cause contact dermatitis and is also toxic to cattle.

Dutchman's Breeches

Dicentra cucullaria (L.) Bernh.

Family: *Fumariceae*
Fumitory family

Additional names:
colic weed, Indian boys and girls, kitten breeches, monks hood, staggerweed

These intricate flowers have sparked imaginative names in scientific and common forms. A glance at the curious, pendulous flowers will show why it is called *dutchman's breeches*. Its complicated and unusual petal structure also gives rise to both the genus and species names. *Dicentra* is the Greek for two-spurred, meaning the spurs that form the legs of the breeches. These are part of the two outer petals that have a large pouch at their base. *Cucullaria* is from the Latin for hooded. It refers here to the tips of a pair of inner petals that are spoon shaped and joined at the top to form a protective hood over the inner parts of the flower, the anthers and the stigma.

Flowers with such complicated structures have usually evolved in response to their mechanism of pollination. This is true of dutchman's breeches, which is pollinated by bumblebees. The light color and the conspicuous, pendulous position of the showy flowers attract the bees. They land on the flowers and hang on to them while they begin to probe for nectar. These bees are strong enough to force their way into the opening between the inner and outer petals, first on one side and then on the other. This moves the hinged upper part of the inner petals and exposes the stamens and stigma. As the bees forage for the nectar produced in the spur, they are well dusted with pollen from the stamens. After they have removed nectar from both sides of the flower, they inadvertently carry the pollen from it to the next flower they visit. The pollen from one flower will not fertilize its own ovules. So dutchman's breeches depends on this action of bees to cross-pollinate it, thus producing seed.

Dutchman's breeches roots are a scaly cluster of tubers. They are usually pink to red in appearance because they are covered with minute red dots. These roots have often been used in folk medicine to treat urinary problems and as a poultice for skin disease. The roots are also slightly poisonous when eaten. Several toxic alkaloids have been found in the roots of dutchman's breeches.

The familiar garden flower bleeding heart is also a member of the genus *Dicentra (D. spectabilis)* and is a rare species found on rocky slopes from western New York State south to Georgia.

Squirrel Corn

**Dicentra
canadensis
(Goldie) Walp.**

Family: *Fumariaceae*
Fumitory family

Additional names:
staggerweed, turkey corn

The finely cut, lacy, bluish green leaves of squirrel corn and dutchman's breeches, both species of *Dicentra,* look alike. However, their flower and root structures are different. The common name *squirrel corn* refers to the plant's root, which resembles a large grain of corn. It has numerous, small yellow to pale brown tubers that are not clustered as they are in dutchman's breeches. The flowers of squirrel corn have outer petals with shorter, inwardly rounded spurs and a conspicuously crested inner pair of petals, all of which differ from dutchman's breeches. The flowers are also highly scented, with a hyacinthlike fragrance that attracts the bee pollinators.

Squirrel corn, like dutchman's breeches, occurs in rich woods from New England to North Carolina and west to Mississippi. As is a common feature with plants that share the same pollinator, it flowers one or two weeks later than dutchman's breeches so that their flowering period in any single area only just overlaps. The competition between them is reduced by this sequential flowering, and the available food resources of nectar and pollen for insects are spread out over a longer period.

Pollen and nectar are not the only foods that this species provides as "payment" for the services of insects. Plants must distribute their seeds to ensure future generations, and this species is unusual because it depends on ants for seed dispersal. At the base of each seed of squirrel corn is a spongy, yellowish white mass called an elaiosome (oil body). This fat- and oil-rich tissue is ideal food for ants, who carry the seeds to their nest. They eat the elaisome but not the seed. Since the smooth, round seeds are hard for ants to hold in their mandibles, they drop many on the way to their nest and so spread the seeds of squirrel corn around the forest floor, where they will later germinate.

Like dutchman's breeches, squirrel corn has been quite widely used in folk medicine. It contains several toxic alkaloids, including corydine and the hallucinogenic bulbocapnine. One alkaloid, cryptopine, has a slowing action on the heart myocardium but has not been used by modern medicine.

The common name *staggerweed* that has been given to *Dicentras* comes from their potent effect on cattle. They are toxic to cattle and can cause them to stagger around as if drunk, have convulsions, and occasionally die.

Sessile-leaved Bellwort

**Uvularia
sessilifolia
L.**

Family: *Liliaceae*
Lily family

Additional names:
straw lily, wild oats

This is an early spring flower of the shadiest parts of the forest. It is found in rich woodlands from New Brunswick to Georgia. The name *sessilifolia* refers to the way the leaves grow without leafstalks or petioles. They are attached directly to the stem and so are called sessile leaves. Each plant bears a single, delicate, bell-shaped flower, which has given the plant the name bellwort. Sometimes it is called *straw lily,* which must refer to its straw-colored flowers. This plant is sometimes cultivated as an ornamental in woodland gardens.

The mucilaginous roots of this species were used by various Indian groups as a calmant and for the treatment of rattlesnake bites. The Ojibwe used the root for the treatment of stomach complaints. They also used it as part of their hunting potion to attract deer bucks.

Mayapple

Podophyllum peltatum L.

Family: *Berberidaceae Barberry family*

Additional names:
American mandrake, devil's apple, duck's foot, raccoon berry, wild lemon

The medicinal uses of the mayapple are documented over many centuries. The Meskwaki Indians used it for the treatment of snake bites. Other tribes used it to treat warts and to kill parasitic worms. Because its root resembled the unrelated mandrake root, an important medicinal plant, the mayapple was popular among the early colonists. It has been used as a cathartic, emetic, to remove warts, and to treat syphilis.

Modern research has proved again with the mayapple that folk medicine often had value. The mayapple's roots and leaves are poisonous, but they contain the substance podophyllotoxin, which has been shown to be active against various types of cancer. A derivative of this resin has now been introduced for the treatment of testicular cancer under the trade name Vepeside. The mayapple has proved to be one of the most important plants so far known for the treatment of cancer.

The mayapple occurs from Quebec to Florida and west to Texas. It is a familiar sight in spring as the underground perennial rhizomes send up a mass of erect stems, each bearing one or two umbrellalike, peltate leaves. Peltate leaves are ones in which the stalk is attached to the middle of the blade rather than at the extreme end of the tapered leaf. This is followed by solitary, creamy white flowers that are two to three inches in diameter. The ripe fruits are yellow and resemble small lemons. They are edible once they are fully ripe and are sometimes used in preserves.

31

Wild Strawberry

Fragaria virginiana Miller

Family: *Rosaceae Rose family*

Additional names: *scarlet strawberry, Virginia strawberry*

The very name *wild strawberry* evokes the magic of surprise. The creamy white flowers, with their simple, rounded petals and bright yellow stamens, peep up from the creeping leaves. A few weeks later miniature strawberries have formed, and the fragile petals have blown away in the wind. As the tiny fruit is held up to the sun it gradually loses its greenness, turns cream colored and speckled with seeds, and finally, as if absorbing the warmth and color of the setting sun, it sparkles red. There it hides, fragrant and bright, its seeds embedded in pits in its skin as if waiting to be found and bring delight.

It is a fruit that was used on both sides of the Atlantic before the modern domesticated one was produced. Europeans originally cultivated the woodland strawberry *(Fragaria vesca)* and Indians from Canada to Chile ate the fruits of American species and in some cases domesticated them. The scarlet or wild strawberry is the species of eastern North America and ranges from Labrador to Georgia and from Alaska to California.

The domestic strawberry originated as a hybrid between the scarlet strawberry and *Fragaria chiloensis,* a Chilean species. These two species were introduced to France, where in the mid-eighteenth century a natural hybrid was found with unusually large, fragrant fruits. It had originated from a plant of *F. chiloensis* pollinated by *F. virginiana.* The Chilean species was cultivated for its fruit by the Mapuche and Huilliche Indians of Chile, so it was already a domesticated species in its own right, but its qualities were greatly improved by crossing it with the familiar wild strawberry of North America.

Indigenous peoples throughout the range of the wild strawberry have used it for food and medicine. The root is noted for its astringent effect on various stomach complaints.

Ground Ivy

Glechoma hederacea L.

Family: *Lamiaceae Mint family*

Additional names: *ale hoof, gill-over-the-ground, hay maids, hedge maids, lizzy-run-up-the-ledge, tunhoof*

This small, creeping plant trails along the ground like ivy and puts up short, upright trailing branches. It is a native of Europe and was introduced in the New World by the colonists. It, too, has been a successful colonist in America and now occurs from Ontario and Newfoundland to Georgia and Alabama and west to Missouri and Kansas.

Sometimes this plant has been placed in the catnip genus, *Nepeta,* but the axillary flowers distinguish it from catnip. The catnips have flowers at the end of the stem and branches, rather than at the junction of the leaves and stem.

The common names are rich with history. The leaves are reminiscent of those of ivy, which led to its usual common name of *ground ivy;* the name *gill-over-the-ground* comes from the French *guiller* (to ferment), since the leaves were used by the Saxons to flavor and clarify their beer before hops were introduced. In Britain gill tea was made by infusing the leaves in boiling water and honey or sugar. It was used as a remedy for coughs. Later, because gill also meant a girl, this plant became known as *hedge maids.* In North America, only the name ground ivy is used commonly.

> *The women of our Northerne parts, especially Wales and Cheshire, do turn Herbe Ale-hoof into their Ale—but the reason I know not. It also purgeth the head from rheumaticke humors flowing from the braine.*
>
> Gerarde, *Herbal*

This plant is mentioned by many other herbalists as a cure for many ailments. Its use spread to North America, where a tea of the leaves was made and drunk cold by painters to prevent lead sickness and cure lead poisoning. The tea was also used as an eyewash.

33

Rhodora

Rhododendron canadense L.

Family: *Ericaceae*
Heath family

Additional name:
Canadian rhodora

This wild member of the *Azalea* and *Rhododendron* genus grows as a low shrub on acid soils in bogs, on wet slopes, and on rocky summits that range from Newfoundland and eastern Quebec to northern New Jersey and Pennsylvania.

Rhodora, whose name is derived from the Greek word for rose, *rodon* (referring to the color of the flower), has attractive and conspicuous flowers. They are clusters of pinkish lavender, which show up well because the blossoms open before the leaves are fully unfolded, when little else is in flower. The curving petals and long stamens of the flowers, set on the ends of branches, give the impression of a delicately hovering bird or butterfly.

The journal of the New England Botanical Club is appropriately named *Rhodora* after this plant, one of the most attractive of the regional flora.

Dandelion

Taraxacum
officinale
(L.) Weber

Family: *Asteraceae*
Aster family

Additional names:
*priests crown, swine's
snout*

The brilliant yellow dandelion is known to countryman, suburbanite, and city dweller, to adult and child. Its familiarity comes from its resourceful ways of responding to difficulties. In the first place, it produces a long, deep taproot that retains the ability to produce a new plant if the leaves, and even part of the root, are pulled up. Then its flower stalk behaves in an original way. It grows very fast when the flower bud is almost ready to open. The yellow head catches the sunlight, ripens, and returns to a budlike shape. Then the stalk retracts to protect the forming seeds. When they are mature it returns to full height, lifting up to the wind not the golden head, but a silvery ball of down made of about two hundred tiny parachutes, each carrying a seed. As the wind blows, the parachutes float off to become new plants, each tiny seed already programmed to repeat the complex cycle of life.

The dandelion weed is a useful plant. Italians and Greeks have a special taste for the rather bitter young leaves, which are sold in bunches in ethnic markets of New York City. Dandelion salad is both tasty and nutritious, as the dandelion leaf contains ten times the amount of vitamin A as lettuce, as well as more vitamin C, iron, and protein. Vineland, New Jersey, the dandelion-growing capital of the United States, produces them as a commercial crop. The roots are often ground and pulverized to make dandelion coffee, which when well prepared is hard to distinguish from real coffee. A delicious wine can be made from freshly opened flowers, and a yellow dye for wool can be extracted from its flowers and roots.

The Latin and common names tell us about its characteristics and uses. *Dandelion* comes from the French *dent de lion* (lion's tooth), a phrase reflected in Linnaeus's original name, *Leontodon*. *Swine's snout* comes from the shape of the forming seed head, which is bulbous at the base and then tapers into a snout. The generic name comes from the Greek words *taraxos* (disorder) and *akos* (remedy), which along with the specific name *officinale* indicates medicinal usage. It is recorded as a medicine in the writings of Arabian physicians of the tenth century. Since then herbals have recorded many ways in which to use the dandelion as a tonic or diuretic, for the treatment of liver diseases, and for use against many kinds of stomach ailments. It is probably most used as a diuretic.

Large-flowered Trillium

***Trillium grandiflorum* (Michx.) Salisb.**

Family: *Liliaceae*
Lily family

Additional names:
giant white trillium, trinity lily, wake-robin

The pure and simple shape of the white trillium is perfect. Three large white petals, each deeply veined and lightly frilled around the edge, contrast with the green three-leafed whorl below them; a trinity of white above a trinity of green.

A drift of green and white often lies on the floor of the woods, as these plants spread naturally in shaded and open woodlands.

This is a wide-ranging species that occurs from Quebec to Florida and Georgia. It occurs on acid and alkaline soils, which makes it easy to grow in cultivation.

The white trillium has many variations in leaf and petal shape, petal color (aging flowers turn pink), and even in the number of floral parts and leaves. The double-flowered forms with multiple petals have often been taken into cultivation. Other forms have long-stalked leaves that are borne lower on the stem than normal. Another aberrant type has petals with green stripes toward the flower centers. This has led to the description of many forms, some of which have been given scientific names, adding to the confusion about the definition of this species.

The roots of most species of *Trillium* have been used in folk medicine. The white trillium has been particularly important by virtue of its widespread distribution. The root is highly astringent and has been used as an expectorant, as a tonic, and to stop bleeding.

Solomon's Seal

Polygonatum biflorum (Walt.) Ell.

Family: *Liliaceae*
Lily family

Additional names:
sealwort, smooth Solomon's seal

The imaginative common name of this plant, Solomon's seal, comes about because it has a fleshy underground rhizome, which puts up a new shoot at its apex each spring. Each fall, the stem dies back to the root after bearing the leaves and flowers, and it leaves a scar. These annual scars, which can be counted to determine the age of the plant, resemble a seal with an **S**, such as those used with wax in the olden days to seal mail. The Latin name also refers to the appearance of the rhizome and is derived from the Greek words *polus,* meaning many, and *gonu,* a knee or joint.

This is a common plant in woods and thickets from southern Canada to Florida and west to Texas. It reaches about three feet in height, while its close relatives, the giant Solomon's seal, can attain eight feet under good conditions. From May to July it can be recognized by its paired flowers *(biflorum),* which hang, often concealed, on slender stalks under the leaves where they join the stem. After bees pollinate the flowers, dark blue berries form.

The root of this species was eaten as a survival food by the Iroquois and other Indian tribes. They have also been used medicinally in various ways. The British herbalist John Gerard wrote of the European Solomon's seal:

> *The root of Solomon's seal stamped while it is fresh and greene, and applied, taketh away in one night, or two at the most, any bruise, black and blew spots gotten by falls or womans wilfulnesse, in stumbling upon their hasty husbands fists or such like.*

The crushed roots were widely used as a poultice for wounds and skin inflammations.

Mayflower

Maianthemum canadense Desf.

Family: *Liliaceae*
Lily family

Additional names:
Canada mayflower, two-leaved Solomon's seal, wild lily of the valley

This delicate white-flowered plant does look like a wild lily of the valley as it carpets the woodland floors. Unlike the lily of the valley, it has eighteen to twenty flowers on each cluster, and the flowers do not hang down. When they are fully open these tiny flowers look like stars, with their long stamens standing out beyond the petals. Each plant bears one inflorescence on the same main stem as the leaves. Often the stem is angled at the junction with each leaf so it is rather zigzagged. It spreads by its underground root systems, so it is not dependent on any bird or animal to disperse its seeds. Berries still form, however—red, white, or mottled in color—and they provide food for creatures in autumn.

The specific name *canadense* is applied to several plants in this book named for Canada because the material studied by the original author of the species came from Canada. Mayflower occurs from Labrador south to Georgia and west to South Dakota, so it is not a specifically Canadian plant.

Mayflower can easily be confused with three-leaved Solomon's seal, but it differs in its four, rather than six, petals, and the leaves are rounded, not pointed, at the junction with the stem. Its similarity to Solomon's seal is reflected in the name it is often given: *two-leaved Solomon's seal.*

The Ojibwe Indians use this plant to maintain kidney function during pregnancy and as a cure for sore throat and headache.

41

Jack-in-the-Pulpit

Arisaema triphyllum (L.) Schott

Family: *Araceae Arum family*

Additional names: *bog onion, brown dragon, cuckoo-pint, devil's ear, dragon root, Indian turnip, lords and ladies, marsh pepper, starchwort, wake-robin, wild pepper, wild turnip*

A compact green shoot advances the return of the jack-in-the-pulpit. The leaves, growing out of the flat underground corm, are tightly rolled around the flower bud. Gradually it unfurls one or two leaf stems, each with three leaflets. The third stem carries a hooded green-purple spathe, or modified leaf, typical of this plant family. This spathe forms the pulpit. It is funnellike, with an opening in the front and a flap bent over the top like a sound box on a cathedral pulpit. "Jack" is the sheltered spadix, a candlelike structure that stands erect in the center. The flowers are at the base of the spadix.

Jack does not exhibit the behavior of a normal preacher since he changes sex from time to time during his twenty years of life! Quite recently scientists have found that, depending on the amount of food stored in the underground corm as reserves for the winter, it will send up either male or female flowers. When the reserves are small, the plant will produce a single leaf and male flowers, which require less energy than female flowers that must then produce seeds. (It demands less energy to produce sperm than a baby.) In years when the plant has sufficient energy stored, there will be two leaves and the flowers will be female. Some years there is a male preacher in the pulpit, and other years a female.

In the inflorescences with female flowers, the spathe withers and the lower portion of the spadix remains. The fertilized flowers develop into green berries that ripen to an attractive bright red by August.

Jack-in-the-pulpit occurs from New Brunswick to South Carolina and west to Minnesota and Kansas. As some of the common names imply, the corms were a common food of the Indians. However, they must never be eaten raw because the calcium oxalate crystals they contain are similar to those of dumb cane. The Indians boiled the corms and changed the water several times before eating them. Several medicinal uses of jack-in-the-pulpit are recorded, such as those of the Pawnee Indians who pulverized the dried roots and dusted the powder on their heads to relieve headaches, and the Mohawk who considered it an effective contraceptive.

43

Corn Lily

**Clintonia
borealis
(Ait.) Raf.**

Family: *Liliaceae
Lily family*

Additional names:
*bluebead, dog berry, heal
all, northern lily, wild
corn yellow clintonia*

This attractive spring flower was named in honor of one of the former governors of New York State, DeWitt Clinton (1769–1828).

In May or June it produces three to eight corn yellow flowers that are borne well above the leaves on a six- to eight-inch flower stalk. Below the flower are the two to five stemless tapered leaves with the parallel venation that is characteristic of members of the lily family and most other monocotyledonous plants. The beauty of this plant continues after flowering when the fruits mature into bright, cobalt blue berries, giving it the local name *bluebead.*

This species occurs from Labrador and Newfoundland south to Tennessee and Georgia wherever there are conifer forests. The leaves and flowers arise from a deeply buried bulb that allows the plant to survive the winter cold in the forest.

It is not surprising that this plant has been used in folk medicine because the steroid compound diosgenin used in birth-control pills has been found in small quantities in the roots. Fortunately the species is unlikely to be overused for the extraction of diosgenin because this compound is more easily extracted from a Mexican species of yam. The plant is mildly poisonous, and the name *dog berry* arose from the ancient belief that dogs used it to poison their teeth so that they could kill their prey!

Virginia Cowslip

**Mertensia
virginica
(L.) DC.**

Family: *Boraginaceae
Borage family*

Additional names:
*bluebells, mertensia,
Virginia bluebell*

Virginia cowslip occurs over a wide area of North America. It is found from southern Ontario to North Carolina, and west to Minnesota and Nebraska. It is most common in the moist woodland and in shady places along streams and on wet hillsides, particularly in the midwest. There it often blankets the earth with blue in springtime.

It has a fleshy rootstock from which the blue-tinged leaf buds emerge in April. These unfurl quickly and flowering stems soon follow.

The flower buds are a cluster of delicate pink, but as the flowers open they become pale blue. They are shaped like tiny trumpets and keep thin nectar high up inside the closed tube. This means it can only be reached by hummingbirds and long-tongued bumblebees. It flowers over several weeks, but after the seeds have formed the whole visible plant dies down, usually by June, and only the rootstock maintains its life underground.

Many species of *Mertensia* have been brought into cultivation, including the Virginia cowslip. In cultivation it has the advantages of flowering in several weeks and then dying back after flowering.

45

Pink Lady's Slipper

Cypripedium acaule Ait.

Family: *Orchidaceae Orchid family*

Additional names: *moccasin flower, nerve root, squirrel's shoes, stemless lady, two-lips*

The pink lady's slipper plant graces the woods of New England in different ways throughout the seasons. In spring the fresh green leaves form a protective shelter around the emerging flower stalk. By late May or early June the ornate, deep pink, veined flower hangs from the firm straight stem, with its green-brown upper petals and sepals stretched fingerlike above its head. Small seeds drop from the seedpods late in the summer, but the pods and stem remain, brown and erect, marking their woodland place, gentle reminders of the hidden life of the root below the ground preparing for another spring.

This lovely flower depends upon the bumblebee to assist it in producing seeds. Bumblebees force their way into the pouch through the crack that extends along its upper side. In their search for footing, they pollinate the flower by touching exactly the right places. Sometimes bees cut their way out of the bottom of the flower rather than refinding the slit through which they entered. The seedpods mature in late summer, and the numerous small seeds are released.

The pink lady's slipper was named *acaule,* or stemless, by Aiton because the leaves are produced in a cluster on the surface of the ground rather than on a leafstalk. The flower stalk grows out of the center of the two or more leaves.

This is a widespread species that occurs in a wide range of habitats on acid soil varying from the border of swamps to dry woodland and even sand dunes. It is commonest as a woodland plant in pine forests. Its range extends from Newfoundland and Alberta to New Jersey and northern Indiana and further south to Alabama along the mountains and coastal dunes.

The roots have often been used in folk medicine, especially for the treatment of nervous disorders and stomach problems. For this reason, like the yellow lady's slipper, it is sometimes known as *nerve root.*

Sheep Sorrel

**Rumex acetosella
L.**

Family: *Polygonaceae
Buckwheat family*

Additional name:
field sorrel

Sheep sorrel is a native of Europe and Asia that has become naturalized over most of North America. It is found in rocky and waste places and in short grassland where the soil is acid. It grows from six to twelve inches tall. Once it is established, it forms large mats because of its creeping perennial rootstocks. At times it tinges a whole meadow or hillside with red because the entire plant can be red when it grows in particularly poor soil. The flower branches bear either male or female flowers, depending on the gender of the plant. This phenomenon, called dioecism, ensures cross-fertilization between plants. Both the male and female flowers are very small and inconspicuous. The male flowers hang down on short, jointed stalks. Bees and small butterflies visit both the male and female flowers for pollen and so pollinate the female flower, which then bears fruit. The leaves are of a characteristic arrowhead shape.

The name *sorrel* is derived from an Anglo-Saxon word meaning sour, with the diminutive *-el* as suffix. Oxalic acid gives the plant a sour taste. It has been used in salads and in cooking, but this is inadvisable due to the high quantity of oxalates, which can cause kidney stones to form. Sheep sorrel has also been used as a medicinal plant, mainly for the treatment of sores and tumors. The leaves contain a high quantity of vitamin A.

Sheep sorrel belongs to the large dock genus *Rumex*.

Wild Columbine

**Aquilegia
canadensis
L.**

Family: *Ranunculaceae
Buttercup family*

Additional names:
*bells, Canadian
columbine, cluckies,
honeysuckle, meeting
houses, rock-bells,
rock lily*

The wild columbine is so graceful and elegant that it was introduced to Europe from North America, unlike many plants that were transferred from east to west with the colonizers. We have records that the naturalist John Tradescant (1608–1662), the royal gardener, obtained it from Virginia for King Charles I. Since the various species of columbine readily hybridize, many garden hybrids have been produced.

This is a species of rocky woodland and open places; its range extends from Newfoundland and Saskatchewan to Texas and Florida. The stems can grow up to six feet tall, and the nodding scarlet and yellow flowers adorn the top of the stalk. The leaves of this plant are compound—that is, each leaf is divided into a number of leaflets. The leaves are twice divided into series of three, and each one is three lobed. The flowers have a scarlet exterior but are yellow within. There are five red spurs, or nectar tubes, which extend backward from the center of the flower. The nectar is at the base of the spur and can be obtained only by long-tongued bees that search for it and also pollinate the flowers.

The European columbine features in many plays and books. William Shakespeare wrote in *Hamlet*: "There's fennel for you and columbine." The columbine in Ophelia's hand is significant as it is the symbol of the ingratitude of which she is being accused.

The root of columbine contains a number of alkaloids such as aquilegine, berberine, and magnoflorine. These components have made the columbines important in folk medicine and also make the plant poisonous.

49

Yellow Lady's Slipper

***Cypripedium calceolus* L. variety *pubescens* (Willd.) Correll**

Family: *Orchidaceae Orchid family*

Additional names:
American valerian, Indian shoe, nerve root, whip-poor-will's shoe, yellows

The lady's slipper orchids are among the most popular plants of the New England flora. The yellow species, which flowers in May and June, is one of the most attractive. Its stem is from nine to twenty-five inches tall, with paired leaves wrapped around the base and one or two slipperlike flowers on the central stem. The "toes" of the slipper flowers are usually purple veined; this part of an orchid flower is called the labellum. Bees visiting the flowers get inside the labellum and cannot exit the way they entered and so have to press their way out by the opening at the base or in some cases cut their way out. In so doing they brush against the stigma and anthers, pollinating the flower. The sticky pollen easily adheres to the bees. Unlike most orchids, the yellow lady's slipper's pollen is in loose grains not in a pollen mass or pollinia.

This plant is sometimes called *American valerian* or *nerve root* because of its medicinal properties. The roots were used in the same way as those of valerian: to treat hysteria, as a nervous stimulant, and as an antispasmodic. The roots were used by many Indian groups for a variety of ailments. The Ojibwe used them as a remedy for female troubles of all kinds.

This plant occurs rarely but over a large area, from Newfoundland to the Rockies and south to Louisiana and Alabama. The lady's slipper orchids are often picked, but because they are not common they should be left in the forests to produce seeds for future generations. There is also another good reason to avoid picking them: they can provoke an allergic reaction similar to that of poison ivy. Some people react to the sensitizing quinone that is present in all species of lady's slipper, including the beautiful showy lady's slipper *(Cypripedium reginae)*. People who have tried to transplant lady's slippers to their gardens often conclude that there must have been poison ivy growing next to the orchid, but little do they know that their dermatitis was caused by the lady's slipper itself.

Wild Sarsaparilla

Aralia nudicaulis L.

Family: *Araliaceae Ginseng family*

Additional names: *false sarsaparilla, rabbit root, shot bush, small spikenard, wild licorice*

This plant is a herbaceous perennial. It has a long, horizontally creeping rhizome that puts out a single, large compound leaf with three to five finely toothed leaflets. The flowering stem is solitary and leafless, hence the species name *nudicaulis,* meaning naked stem. At the top of this stem is an umbrellalike cluster, or umbel, of greenish white flowers. This umbel type of inflorescence is characteristic of the ginseng family and the closely related parsley, or Umbelliferae, family. The fruits are small black berries resembling buckshot.

As the name *wild sarsaparilla* would imply, this plant has been used in medicine in a similar way to the sarsaparilla, which is not a close relative. True sarsaparilla comes from a tropical species of catbrier *(Smilax)* in the lily family. The name comes from Mexico: *zarza,* meaning a bramble, and *parra,* a vine. Sarsaparilla has long been used as a treatment for syphilis, as a tonic, and as a flavor for food and carbonated drinks. The wild sarsaparilla has roots with a spicy taste and an agreeable, aromatic smell and has consequently been used as a substitute for the true product, both medicinally and in homemade root beer. Its uses arose from Native American traditions. For example, the Cree Indians called it rabbit root and used it for topical application on skin wounds, as well as for the treatment of syphilis. The Ojibwe pounded the fresh root and used it as a poultice to bring a boil to a head.

The range of the wild sarsaparilla reaches from Newfoundland to British Columbia and south to Florida through Alabama and Louisiana. It is quite common in shady places, in moist or dry woodland.

53

Bullhead Lily

***Nuphar
variegatum
Engelm. ex
Durand***

Family: *Nymphaeaceae
Water lily family*

Additional names:
*beaver root, spatterdock,
yellow pond lily, yellow
water lily*

Throughout the summer these lovely plants, with their yellow cupped flowers and heart-shaped leaves, float serenely on ponds and still waters. It is the most common of the northeastern United States pond lilies and is found from Labrador and Newfoundland south to Delaware and west to Kansas and Idaho.

Its heart-shaped leaves and flattened or narrowly winged leaf stem differentiate the bullhead lily from the closely related common spatterdock *(N. advena)*, which usually has leaves raised above the water and a rounded leafstalk.

Water lilies grow with their roots immersed in water buried in oxygen-free sediment. In order for the oxygen to move from the leaves, where it enters the plants, to the roots, there is an internal network of air space with a pressurized flow system that forces the oxygen to the rhizome. This sophisticated mechanism was discovered by scientist John W. H. Dacey, at the Kellog Biological Station in Michigan. He wrote an interesting paper on the subject entitled "Internal Winds in Water-lilies."

Many groups of Indians ate the rhizomes of the yellow water lily. They were boiled well and said to taste like sheep liver. The rhizomes were also used by the Iroquois to make a type of bread. The powdered roots were also used by the Menominee for poultices to heal cuts and reduce swellings.

55

Comfrey

**Symphytum
officinale
L.**

Family: *Boraginaceae
Borage family*

Additional names:
*ass ear, blackwort,
boneset, bruiseweed,
bruisewort, consolida,
consound, gum-plant,
knitbone, slippery root*

Comfrey is probably an Asian species that was transported throughout Europe by the Romans. Anyone who has experimented with comfrey in the garden can attest to its vigorous growth and that once it is established it is hard to eradicate. Because it is adaptable, it became established throughout Europe. The early colonists planted comfrey at Salem and on Boston Common, and it is now common in New England.

Comfrey's history as a medicinal plant is as long and various as its geographical history. In 400 B.C. Herodotus recommended comfrey for stanching the flow of blood. Since that time it has been mentioned in almost all European writings about medicinal plants. *Boneset,* one of its names, comes about because the plant's most common medicinal use is for healing broken bones. The name *comfrey* originated as a corruption of the Latin *confirma,* alluding to the uniting of bones, and its scientific name *Symphytum* is from the Greek *symphyo,* to unite.

The roots, with their abundant mucilage, have been used as a cure for diarrhea and dysentery, and as an expectorant. The leaves are used for sprains, swellings, cuts, and bruises, and a tea was taken for internal bleeding. In addition comfrey has often been used as a potherb, as a substitute for spinach, and as an animal feed. In the late 1970s, a report from Japan showed that when comfrey leaves comprised a third of rats' diets they developed liver cancer, which caused much concern to comfrey users. The presence of pyrrolizidine alkaloids in comfrey was the cause of the rat cancers. There have been no records of human or animal poisoning through the use of comfrey. However, it is probably better not to use comfrey in the form of teas.

Some of comfrey's other names come from its morphological characteristics. It is called *ass ear* because the hairy, dark green leaves have the same shape as an ass's ear. The root has large quantities of mucilage, a fact that gave rise to two other names: *slippery root* and *gum-plant.*

The yellow or purple bell-shaped flowers attract large numbers of bees. The flowers, like those of other members of the Borage family, form a scorpioid inflorescence. This means that the flower branches are curved, with all the flowers growing out of one side of the stem so that they are shaped like a scorpion's tail.

57

Beach Pea

Lathyrus japonicus Willd.

Family: *Fabaceae*
Pea family

Like many seashore plants, the beach pea has a wide distribution. Its seeds are carried from place to place by ocean currents, which is why it occurs on the Pacific Coast, in Japan and Chile, and on other temperate-region shorelines.

This spreading vine with its angled stem is a familiar component of the seashore vegetation. In eastern America it ranges from Labrador and Newfoundland south to New Jersey. It also occurs around the shores of the Great Lakes and other lakes with beaches such as Lake Champlain.

At the base of each compound leaf, consisting of three to six pairs of leaflets, there is a pair of leaflike arrowhead-shaped structures called a stipule. The leaves terminate in a tendril, which is a common modification of leaves in climbing plants. The five to ten purplish pink flowers are borne at the apex of the stem. The flowers have the typical structure of members of the pea family, with a showy upper petal, or standard, and the lower petals forming the boat-shaped keel. Flowering begins in June and continues until the time of the first frost. The slender pods filled with small seeds form quickly after the flower fades.

As with many members of the pea family, the roots of this plant bear nodules that contain nitrogen-fixing bacteria. They are able to fix directly atmospheric nitrogen and make it available to the plant. Nitrogen forms part of the structure of proteins, so it is an essential nutrient for all plants. There is little nitrogen in the poorest of sandy soils on beaches where the beach peas grow, but because they are able to capture it from the atmosphere they can thrive even in such a nutrient-poor habitat.

The young seeds are edible, but they are small and time-consuming to harvest and do not have the sweetness or flavor of the garden pea. Care must be taken not to confuse the beach pea with the perennial pea *(Lathyrus latifolius)*, which has poisonous seeds. The perennial pea is easy to identify by its flat-winged stems and a leaf with only two leaflets.

59

False Solomon's Seal

Smilacina racemosa (L.) Desf.

Family: *Liliaceae*
Lily family

Additional name:
false spikenard

This plant, as its name suggests, superficially resembles Solomon's seal. However, the numerous flowers are borne on long stalks in an alternately branched cluster at the end of the stem rather than directly from the main stem. There are many other floral differences in the much more open flowers of the false Solomon's seal. These differences are so great that it is separated into a different genus of plants. True Solomon's seal has pendulous, bell-like flowers.

False Solomon's seal grows from Nova Scotia and Ontario to Georgia and west to British Columbia and Arizona. It is a widespread and common plant of the woodland and open places on richer soils. Several other related species of *Smilacina* also grow in our region and have names that refer to the similarity to true Solomon's seal. *Smilacina stellata* (L.) Desf. is known as star-flowered Solomon's seal but is a smaller plant with larger flowers growing directly from the main stem. *Smilacina trifolia* (L.) Desf. is known as three-leaved Solomon's seal because it often has three leaves but can vary from two to four.

The roots of the false Solomon's seal have been used frequently in folk medicine.

61

Ragged Robin

**Lychnis
flos-cuculi
L.**

Family: *Caryophyllaceae
Pink family*

Additional names:
*crowflower, cuckoo
flower*

*There with fantastic garlands did she come
Of crow-flowers, nettles, daisies, and long purples . . .*
Hamlet, *IV.vii. 168–169*

The twining of wildflowers to make garlands or chaplets was a charming Elizabethan custom in England. It is referred to in this quotation where Ophelia, sad and demented, had been seen weaving such garlands. Ragged robin, or crowflower, is a native plant of Europe. It also occurs in northern Asia through Siberia and the Caucasus mountains. It has been introduced to the northeastern United States and Canada from Quebec south to Pennsylvania. It has naturalized well in a few places.

The species name, *flos-cuculi,* means cuckoo flower. It has this name in England because it begins to flower at about the same time that the cuckoos arrive back from their winter migration. The genus name is derived from the Greek word *lychnos,* or flame, because of the flower color, although occasionally the flowers are white rather than pink.

The unusual ragged appearance of its vivid pink petals brought it the name of *ragged robin*. Instead of normal, entire, and smooth-margined petals, these are deeply and unevenly divided, so that they look as if they have been torn apart by the wind. This shredded appearance, however, is the natural state for ragged robin.

Wrinkled Rose

Rosa rugosa Thunb.

Family: *Rosaceae*
Rose family

Additional names: *rugosa rose, sand rose, Turkestan rose*

This vivid rose thrives on the beaches and dunes of New England. In fact, it is a native of China and Japan that was introduced to North America, where it has established well. It is used as a garden plant and also has naturalized in both coastal and inland areas from Quebec south to New Jersey and to the West Coast.

This plant is called *wrinkled rose* because of the wrinkled appearance of the leaflets. The botanical term for wrinkled is *rugose,* hence its scientific name.

The sweetly perfumed flowers vary in color from vivid pink to lavender pink, and the stamens form a bright yellow center. The rose can be as large as three inches in diameter. After the petals fall the rose hips form, ripening to a brilliant red. The hips of many roses, including the rugosa rose, are rich in vitamins C and A. They are often used in soups, jellies, baby foods, and syrups. Rose hips are so nutritious that during World War II they were collected in large numbers in Great Britain to make rose-hip syrup as a source of vitamins. I remember as a young schoolchild looking forward to gathering rose hips in the fall as part of the war effort. In Britain we gathered the hips of the dog rose *(Rosa canina),* but all wild species of rose have edible hips. Some are more flavorful and juicy than others. Five mature bushes of wrinkled rose can provide a family of four with enough vitamin C for the entire winter. If you gather rose hips, the best time is in the fall at about the time of the first frost.

Our word *rosary* comes from the custom in medieval Europe of drying rose hips and stringing them together to make prayer beads.

When painting flowers I need not wait for inspiration. They are inspiring enough. Painting them means working on and refining my ability to experience, to feel in depth, and to learn. It is my quiet happiness and also my struggle at times.

SUMMER

The nights are short and warm. The June air is filled with the perfume of freshly mowed grass. Farmer Rogerson and sons are busy raking and baling. And then the sweet smell of hay! The light, tender green of the hills darkens into full and vibrant green.

We don't want to destroy the beautiful, colorful flower carpet in front of our house. And so we mow the grass in little paths through the meadow, leaving the rest the way nature created it. And what a creation! Yellow and orange hawkweed, red and white clover combined with purple knapweed, white oxeye daisies beside sky blue chicory, silvery white yarrow, patches of yellow St. Johnswort, purple vetch and alfalfa, brilliantly scarlet pinks, yellow evening primrose, white bladder campion, yellow cinquefoil, and wood sorrel sprinkled with spectacular pink ragged robin and brilliantly yellow buttercups. Who would ever want to change it all into a lawn? Wild strawberries are ripe and our meadow becomes a banquet hall for us and our friends. Life is so beautiful!

In July the days and nights are hot. We are longing to swim in the refreshing waters of ponds and lakes, which are decorated with spectacular golden heads of bullhead lilies. Later they give their place to magical fragrant water lilies, also arrowhead, pickerelweed, and bladderwort.

Our woods give us shelter to hide from the heat. There I can also find flowers, even though not too many want to grow in the shade. They reflect the mystery of the forest. Indian pipe is all white and almost transparent without any chlorophyll. A strong, sweet perfume stops me on one of my mushroom-picking expeditions, and my nose leads me to a mysterious place between maples and spruces, where I find a stunning, tall plant with delicately cut flowers: purple fringed orchid. The whole atmosphere is so magical, I have to think of fairies.

I also collect herbs and flowers for our daily use. St. Johnswort and yarrow I can pick just in our meadow. Peppermint grows in the nearby creek on the other side of the road. I dry them all and mix them with pineapple weed into delicious teas.

Friendly, fragrant milkweed rims the edges of the roads and meadows. Its young sprouts are so delicious in the spring, and now we collect the young, tender seedpods as a tasty vegetable. We share this food with beautiful yellow-, white-, and black-striped monarch butterfly caterpillars, which live on milkweed leaves. But unlike them, we eat our vegetables cooked.

It is not easy to paint the flowers in hot weather. When I start to work, however, I quickly forget any physical discomfort. But the flowers can't forget theirs, and they wilt very fast. Our refrigerator prolongs their life and helps me to finish my paintings.

I never use photographs. The real flowers breathe life that can never be captured in a photograph. But photographs of flowers don't move, open, or close their blossoms; don't wilt; don't turn their heads to the light. The price for painting live flowers is high but rewarding; when I look at my paintings I can still feel the flowers that lived in front of me.

Anna Vojtech

Mountain Laurel

Kalmia latifolia L.

Family: *Ericaceae Heath family*

Additional names: *calico bush, clamoun, ivy bush, mountain ivy, spoon wood, wood laurel*

The Indians called this shrub *spoon wood* because they used its dense, hard, brown wood to make their eating implements. Later, the early settlers renamed this plant for the plant it most resembled in Europe; the dark evergreen leaves reminded them of laurel. So, although the mountain laurel is not really a laurel but rather a member of the heath or azalea family, it is commonly known as mountain laurel.

The *Kalmias* were named after the Swedish botanist and explorer Peter Kalm. In 1750 he sent specimens of mountain laurel to his fellow countryman and mentor, Linnaeus. Because this species is wide leaved in comparison to the sheep laurel, Linnaeus named it *latifolia,* or broad leaved.

The mountain laurel is the state flower of Connecticut. One of the earliest plant protection laws in the United States (1920) was the Connecticut "laurel law," enacted to protect their state flower.

In spite of its beauty, the mountain laurel is quite poisonous. Kalm's notes on this plant referred to its poisonous properties.

> *The leaves are poison to some animals and food for others. . . . [Leaves] form the winter food for stags and if killed during the time of feeding and the entrails given to dogs to eat, they become quite stupid, and, as it were intoxicated, and often fall so sick that they seem to be at the point of death, but the people who have eaten the venison have not felt the least inconvenience.*

The leaves and berries are harmful to cattle. In Canada, there have been cases of human poisoning when pheasants that have eaten the berries have been shot and eaten. The Indians used to drink a brew of the leaves to commit suicide.

In spite of this, the powdered leaves have also been used as a medicine for rheumatism.

Canada Anemone

**Anemone
canadensis
L.**

Family: *Ranunculaceae
Buttercup family*

The Canada anemone flowers later than the wood anemone and prefers more open habitats such as sandy shores, wet meadows, and damp prairies. It is widespread from Quebec to West Virginia and west to Missouri and New Mexico and is found in greatest abundance on prairies, where it occurs in large showy colonies.

Many Indian tribes have used it as a medicine. The Chippewa chewed the root to stop internal bleeding and used pieces of root in the nostrils to stop nosebleeds. The Ojibwe also used the root in preparing a cure for sore throats and to clear the throats of singers.

The Canada anemone is an attractive wildflower that also does well in perennial gardens and planted among shrubs and ferns in a semiwild garden.

71

Common Blackberry

Rubus alleghemiensis Porter

Family: *Rosaceae*
Rose family

This is one of the most common of the blackberries. It is found from New Brunswick and Nova Scotia south to Tennessee and North Carolina. Its stems are erect rather than trailing, and they grow from two to nine feet long. The prickles on the stems are erect and not hooked, as in some other species. The flower stalks are covered with gland-tipped hairs.

The fruit is a sweet and pleasant-tasting blackberry consisting of many globules, each derived from a single carpel and fused together.

The blackberry belongs to a large genus of plants that includes many with edible fruits, such as the raspberry, dewberry, and loganberry. The fruits have long been used for jellies, pies, and preserves, and as a source of dye. The root and the green branches also yield a black dye that has been used to dye wool and silk and even hair. Since the root is also a strong astringent, it has also been used extensively in traditional medicine for the treatment of diarrhea and other stomach ailments.

The Iroquois Indians made use of the blackberry and raspberry. They used them either fresh or dried to make a drink called *uhiayei,* which was sweetened with maple sugar and was drunk during longhouse ceremonies. The blackberry is a common wild plant of thickets and clearings, and it is cultivated for its edible fruit and as a cover in large gardens.

Smooth Rose

Rosa blanda Ait.

Family: *Rosaceae*
Rose family

Additional name:
meadow rose

This rose is called smooth because it is either completely lacking thorns or has only soft slender prickles toward its base. There are no thorns on the flowering stems or on the hips.

The smooth rose is native to North America and occurs in dry woods and on dunes and prairies from Quebec and Manitoba south to New York, Indiana, and Missouri. It has pink flowers that are solitary or in small groups.

The Ojibwe Indians used to soak the root of the smooth rose in warm water and use this infusion as a medicine for inflamed eyes. The stem of the rose hip was used by the Meskwaki to make a remedy for itches.

Yellow Goat's Beard

Tragopogon pratensis L.

Family: *Asteraceae*
Aster family

Additional names:
jack-go-to-bed-at-noon, meadow salsify, noon flower

Yellow goat's beard is another European plant that was introduced to North America in colonial times. It has naturalized widely in Canada and the United States, from Nova Scotia south to Georgia. This attractive relative of the hawkweeds is found mainly in waste places and fields.

Its habits were noted by Cowley in a poem.

The goat's beard, which each morn abroad does peep
But shuts its flowers at noon and goes to sleep.

And as he says, its golden yellow dandelionlike inflorescences open at dawn and close before noon, a custom that gives it the name *jack-go-to-bed-at-noon*. After flowering the tightly closed remnants of the flower expand and flower leaves elongate until a familiar dandelionlike ball of down is produced. During this stage of development the seed ball becomes fluffy and resembles a goat's beard, which gave rise to both the common English name and the scientific name. *Tragopogon* is derived from the Greek words for goat, *tragos*, and beard, *pogon*.

Sometimes the roots of goat's beard comprise a single, central taproot that resembles a thin carrot. It has been used as a survival food in the past.

Sometimes the roots were dug up and dried for use during the winter, and in spring young shoots were used in a similar way to asparagus. In medieval Europe goat's beard was found to be effective for the treatment of urinary infections and kidney stones.

75

Pointed Blue-eyed Grass

***Sisyrinchium angustifolium* Mill.**

Family: *Iridaceae*
Iris family

This low plant, six to eight inches tall, has stiff, erect, and narrow leaves on a twisted stem. It is a tiny relative of the more familiar irises.

The small, violet blue flowers appear to have six petals. However, only three are petals; the other three, in spite of their similar appearance, are sepals. Each flower has a yellow center, or nectar guide, to attract bee pollinators. The combination of grasslike leaves and blue flowers gives rise to its common name.

It is a widely distributed species found from Newfoundland to New York and south along mountains to North Carolina as well as west to Saskatchewan and Kansas. It occurs mainly on hill slopes, dry upland meadows, low woods, and shores.

Sundrops

***Oenothera perennis* L.**

Family: *Onagraceae*
Evening primrose family

Sundrops and the evening primrose both belong to the same genus, *Oenothera*. One wonders then why sundrops open at dawn and close in the evening, just as the flowers of the evening primrose begin to open. The answer is in their relationships with different pollinators. The flowers of sundrops are visited by butterflies and bees, which fly by day, whereas those of the evening primrose attract night-flying hawkmoths.

The seed capsules of sundrops are different from those of the evening primrose, too. They have four wings and an angular shape.

The name *Oenothera* is derived from the Greek words *oenos* (wine) and *thera* (a hunt). It was the name given by Theophrastus to another member of the willow herb family, the roots of which were eaten as an appetizer to prepare the palate for wine.

The word *perennis* in the scientific name of this species is used because it is a perennial plant. The first year it produces a basal rosette of leaves. The flower stalk is produced only in the second and successive years. As the plant grows, other rosettes are formed, and eventually a clump of many rosettes forms with a large number of flowering stems.

This species of sundrops extends in range from Quebec to South Carolina and west to Manitoba. It is the smallest of the three northeastern species and also differs in its small, darker yellow flowers. One of the species of sundrops, *Oenothera pilosella,* is widely cultivated as an ornamental plant in gardens.

Yellow Iris

Iris pseudacorus L.

Family: *Iridaceae Iris family*

Additional names: *daggers, dragon flower, flaggon, fleur-de-luce, fliggers, Jacob's sword, levers, myrtle flag, skeggs, water flag, yellow flag*

Iris, the goddess of the rainbow, lends her name to these flowers because there are many varieties that come in many colors. The more warlike names such as *daggers* and *Jacob's sword* are derived from the bladelike leaves of many iris.

The iris was adopted as a heraldic emblem by King Louis VII of France in his crusade against the Saracens. It then became known as the *fleur de Louis* and soon became corrupted to *fleur-de-luce* and *fleur-de-lys*. Edward III added the fleur-de-lys to the English coat of arms, and it remained there for 250 years. The following Shakespearean quotation refers to its removal.

> *Cropp'd are the flower-de-luces in your arms;*
> *Of England's coat one half is cut away.*
> Henry VI, *Part 1, I.i.80–81.*

Shakespeare was familiar with the flower-de-luces in their heraldic and natural settings. Although it has been naturalized in some places in North America from Newfoundland to Minnesota and far south, it is a native of Europe. It is common beside the river at Stratford-on-Avon, where Shakespeare lived. It thrives in marshy places and adds bright color among the reeds.

These golden flowers are made up of three large petals (standards or flags) and three sepals or falls. The standards rise upward and the falls curve down. The roots of the yellow iris are rich in tannins, which has led to its use as a medicinal plant and dye.

False Hellebore

**Veratrum viride
Ait.**

Family: *Liliaceae
Lily family*

Additional names:

*American veratrum, bear
corn, devil's bite, devil's
tobacco, earth gull,
Indian poke, itch weed,
tickle weed*

The false hellebore has been used both as a poison and as a medicine. The Swedish pioneer naturalist Peter Kalm, after whom the mountain laurel genus *Kalmia* was named, wrote about the use of veratrum to poison and repel birds from cornfields. Grains of corn were boiled with roots of veratrum and put out as bait for birds, which then became intoxicated. When they recovered they never returned to the fields.

The false hellebore is a two- to seven-foot-tall herbaceous perennial with distinctive parallel-veined leaves that clasp the stem. It is a common plant of swamps and wet woods and damp, grassy meadows. It is distributed over an area ranging from Labrador to Maryland and further south to Georgia and Tennessee along mountain ranges, as well as west to Minnesota.

Although poisonous, this species has been used widely as a medicinal plant, as an emetic to cause vomiting, and for the treatment of certain fevers. The roots contain a large variety of toxic alkaloids including germidine and germitrine, which have hypotensive activity.

Some tribes of New England Indians used this plant to test their warriors and future chiefs. They were required to drink a concoction of the roots of false hellebore. If they vomited they were considered weak and therefore unable to lead the tribe. They were given further doses until their body became accustomed to the poison and they no longer vomited. The plant is also toxic to animals, but they usually avoid it because the leaves cause a burning sensation in the mouth.

I paint flower upon flower; every little leaf, fold, each pistil, each cleft and wrinkle of a petal. When first seen, most flowers seem simpler than they really are. Only when I'm actually working on them do I know the tiniest details. I cannot take away from what I see, nor do I feel the need to do so. Nature has no use for my imagination; it is I who must learn from nature. It is like touching the earth itself.

81

Tall Meadow Rue

Thalictrum polygamum Muhl.

Family: *Ranunculaceae*
Buttercup family

Tall meadow rue has two types of flowers on the same plant: male flowers and bisexual flowers. The male flowers have a large number of erect stamens and no pistil, but the bisexual flowers have several pistils and a few stamens.

The flowers form large, sweetly scented clusters that attract great numbers of bees and butterflies. The blue tinge to the leaves is unusual and lends variety in color to the wet meadows, stream banks, and swamps where it grows. It will reach a height of six feet, so it is the tallest of the eastern meadow rues.

It is a common plant found in the area extending from Labrador to Georgia and Tennessee.

Valerian

Valeriana officinalis L.

Family: *Valerianaceae*
Valerian family

Additional names:
all heal, garden heliotrope, setwell

Valerian is nature's own tranquilizer. Its roots contain chemicals called valepotriates, which have sedative and antispasmodic properties. It is one of the plants most used for herbal medicines, as its species name, *officinalis,* testifies. Its genus name, *Valeriana,* derived from the Latin verb *valere* (to be in health), also indicates that it was regarded to have curative properties.

Valerian was extolled by the ancient Greek Dioscorides, who called it *phu.* Perhaps this onomatopoeic name refers to the odor of the drying roots. Some people find this smell repugnant, but others find it not unpleasant. Because of its smell, valerian has been used as an aromatic as well as a medicine. The smell of valerian is as effective as catnip in attracting cats and rats. It has even been said that perhaps the Pied Piper of Hamelin had valerian root in his pockets, and his magic lay not in the sound of his pipe but in the attraction of the smell of the valerian.

Common valerian is a widespread species through Europe and northern Asia, and it grows best on the damp borders of streams and beside ditches. It also occurs in drier, open places. Cultivated and harvested as a medicinal plant in Europe for many centuries, it was brought to North America by early settlers but soon escaped from cultivation and became quite a common plant in New England.

The native swamp valerian of the northeastern United States, *Valeriana uliginosa,* has also been used medicinally, as have many other species of this genus around the world. In addition to the valepotriates and the bad-smelling isovaleric acid, valerians are full of interesting chemicals so it is not surprising that they are important medicinal plants in cultures from Maine to China. *Valeriana sitchensis,* a native of the northwest, is regarded as the most potent medicinal resource of all the species.

The true valerian should not be confused with a species of yellow lady's slipper orchid *(Cypripedium)* that is often called American valerian.

Orange Hawkweed

Hieracium aurantiacum L.

Family: *Asteraceae Aster family*

Additional names: *devil's paintbrush, Grim-the-Collier*

The names *hawkweed* and its Latin equivalent, *Hieracium,* come from an ancient belief that hawks ate these plants to improve their eyesight. The name is derived from the Greek *hieras* (hawk).

In Britain, where it grows abundantly on moors in mining areas, it was called *Grim-the-Collier.* This name was descriptive of the characteristic black, gland-tipped hairs on the green bracts around the flower head. They were obviously thought to resemble the coal dust collected on the clothes of the miners.

Its third name, *devil's paintbrush,* arose because farmers regarded it as an invasive and noxious weed. It is native to Europe. Once it was introduced to America it naturalized and now occurs in fields, forest clearings, and roadsides from Newfoundland and Nova Scotia south to North Carolina and west to Minnesota and Iowa. It is a most attractive plant that grows in dense carpets, adding brilliant color to fields. Its beauty, however, has not endeared it to farmers. A Canadian farmers' circular of 1912 wrote:

> *It is a pernicious weed steadily on the increase. It is utterly useless, spreads rapidly by downy seeds and by runners, finally crowding out all useful plants. . . . Farmers Associations should offer a bonus to boys and girls for a thousand whole plants, roots and all, before they go to seed.*

Although it is a weed, the seeds provide food for birds such as goldfinches, redpolls, and sparrows during the winter months.

Ragged Fringed Orchid

Platanthera lacera (Michx.) G. Don

Family: *Orchidaceae Orchid family*

Additional name: *green fringed orchid*

The ragged petals of many flowers make them attractive, but this has only modest greenish white flowers. Close inspection of the flowers, however, reveals an intricate structure. The lacerated lip is divided into three parts, and above the column there are narrow petals that are entire, not fringed. As in the other fringed orchid flowers, there is a spur that contains the nectar reward for the pollinating moths. This curved spur of the ragged fringed orchid is about half an inch in length.

That this is the most lacerated of all the fringed orchids can be deduced from its Latin name, *lacera,* from the verb *lacere,* meaning to tear. The green fringed orchid is also the commonest of this kind of orchid in the northeastern United States and Canada. It grows from Nova Scotia to Florida and west to Ontario, Texas, and Minnesota. It is a plant of bogs, wet woodlands, meadows, and roadside ditches. In the south it begins to flower in May, but it may flower as late as August in the northern part of its range.

True Forget-Me-Not

Myosotis scorpioides L.

Family: *Boraginaceae Borage family*

The Persian poet Shiras recounts a folktale of an angel who was excluded from paradise because he had fallen in love with a mortal woman. He was not permitted to reenter paradise until his lover had planted the whole earth with forget-me-not flowers. The angel returned to earth to assist her. Hand in hand they completed the task and were both allowed to enter paradise. The woman became an immortal without tasting death and sat by the river of paradise twining forget-me-nots in her hair.

Another similar legend tells of a lover who was once trying to gather these flowers for his sweetheart. He fell into a deep pond. As he was sinking, he cried out, "Forget me not." Then he threw the flowers that were in his hand onto the shore before drowning in the deep water.

The forget-me-not is a favorite European flower that was introduced quickly into the gardens of North America. Since its introduction it has naturalized around lakes, ponds, rivers, and streams throughout the eastern United States and Canada.

The genus name *Myosotis* means mouse ear. It is a reference to the shape and size of the small, fuzzy leaves. The specific name was chosen to describe the flowers. They unfold from a coiled stem that resembles a scorpion's tail, so the name *scorpioides* was used. The flowers are light blue, with a conspicuous yellow eye in the center of the tube. It was from observation of this species that German botanist Christian Konrad Sprengel (1750–1816) discovered that conspicuous, targetlike markings on many flowers serve to guide insects to the nectar. Sprengel was a pioneer in floral biology. Since that time the importance of nectar guides in leading insects to the correct part of the flower to find the nectar and to effect pollination has been widely documented.

When I am at work painting, I release myself from life's daily toil and worries. Even if I have an ear in the children's room and my nose in the kitchen, I nevertheless enjoy at least for a while the beauty of these flowers. I need this beauty for my own feeling of harmony and joy in life.

Spiderwort

Tradescantia virginiana L.

Family: *Commelinaceae*
Spiderwort family

The *Tradescantia*s are named after John Tradescant the elder, gardener, traveler, and plant collector. It was he who introduced spiderwort to the gardens of England about three hundred years ago. It is a popular garden plant because of the deep purplish violet petals of the flowers, which contrast with the conspicuous, yellow stamens. There are color variations in the flowers in the numerous cultivars that now exist. *Tradescantia*s make a good ground cover in moist woods and have the advantage of flowering all summer. The flowers open in early morning and then wilt by noon. After that the petals gradually turn into a jellylike liquid.

Tradescantia is called *spiderwort* because the angular arrangement of the leaves is reminiscent of a squatting spider waiting for its prey.

The natural range is from southern New England south to Georgia and west to Tennessee and Missouri. It is a common plant of roadsides, meadows, and thickets.

Tradescantia is one of the most used plants in modern science. Its chromosomes are large and easy to observe so it is useful for teaching and for experiments with chromosomes, the units of inheritance that contain the genes of an organism. The stamens of this plant are also a favorite in class demonstrations because they consist of a row of linked, thin-walled cells in which the flowing of the cytoplasm (cell contents) from cell to cell is clearly visible.

However, most interesting of all is the sensitivity of the *Tradescantia*s to low-level radiation. The most sensitive is the wandering Jew, a related species, in which the stamens change color when exposed to radiation. The spiderwort was used by NASA and the Soviet space programs in their experiments to test the effects of cosmic radiation on chromosomes. Scientists used pollen mother cells to detect mutations because these are the germ cells that have the potential to transmit genetic defects to the next generation of the plant. By monitoring the effects of radiation on these chromosomes, scientists can estimate the possible effects on human chromosomes.

89

Creeping Bellflower

**Campanula
rapunculoides
L.**

Family: *Campanulaceae
Bellflower family*

Additional names:
*false rampion, roving
bellflower*

Reginald Farrer said of this species, "The most insatiable and irrepressible of beautiful weeds. If once its tall and arching spires of violet bell prevail on you to admit it to your garden, neither you nor its choice inmates will ever know peace again." This European species is another plant that was introduced to gardens of North America because of its beauty. It has blue, bell-shaped flowers but it grows so well that it has escaped and become a weed. It propagates by producing abundant seed and by rhizomes that grow long distances underground and put up suckers some distance from the parent plant. These help to give it an advantage as an invader. It is now distributed from Newfoundland south to West Virginia and west to North Dakota and Missouri.

The species name *rapunculoides* refers to its similarity to another species of bell-flower, the rampion *(Campanula rapunculus),* a much more desirable species for cultivation with beautiful, violet flowers. The name *rapunculus* is a diminutive of *rapa,* or turnip. The roots are still much used as a food in Europe. They are boiled and eaten with a white sauce. The rampion is featured in the Grimms' fairy tale about Rapunzel, who is named after this plant. The plot revolves around the theft of rampions from the garden of a magician.

Shinleaf

Pyrola elliptica Nutt.

Family: *Pyrolaceae*
Wintergreen family

Additional name:
wintergreen

This plant grows in small rosettes of dark evergreen leaves that bring a touch of color to the winter woodlands. In early summer, the stalked flower cluster emerges from the center of the leaf rosettes. It bears very fragrant, greenish white, waxy flowers. Their green-veined petals form a bell.

This is the most common of all the wintergreens, and it grows in dry and moist woods. It is found from Newfoundland to British Columbia and south to Virginia and Ohio. It is closely related to the round-leaved wintergreen *(Pyrola rotundifolia)*, which is a lower plant with more leathery, rounder leaves.

The genus name *Pyrola* is said to be derived from a diminutive of *Pyrus*, the pear, but it is hard to see why.

Partridgeberry

Mitchella repens L.

Family: *Rubiaceae*
Madder family

Additional names:
cat's eyes, checkerberry, deerberry, squaw vine, twin berry, winter clover

This is an attractive creeping plant that trails along the forest floor. It has roots along its stem so it can form large mats. The evergreen leaves have a shiny, dark green surface laced with contrasting white veins.

There are two forms of flowers: one with a long style and short stamens and the other with long stamens and a short style. This phenomenon, heterostyly, ensures cross-pollination. Only pollen from a flower of the opposite morph can germinate and fertilize a flower. The tubular flowers are borne in pairs. After the pair has been pollinated, the ovaries of the two unite to form a scarlet berry. It has two star-shaped scars, or "cat's eyes," marking the position of the sepals of the twin flowers from which the berry was derived. The berries persist all winter and are tasteless but do provide a food for birds.

The partridgeberry grows from Nova Scotia and Ontario to Florida and Texas. It is a common ground cover in woodlands throughout most of the region east of the Mississippi River, and it even extends into Mexico.

Common Wood Sorrel

Oxalis montana Raf.

Family: *Oxalidaceae*
Wood sorrel family

When St. Patrick wanted to illustrate the Christian doctrine of the trinity, he reputedly picked a leaf with three leaflets, which has been known as the shamrock. The identity of the original shamrock has since been debated. Some people believe it was clover; others hold it was the European wood sorrel *(Oxalis acetosella)*, which is closely related to the common wood sorrel of North America. This attractive woodland plant has divided, compound, cloverlike leaves with three heart-shaped leaflets.

The common wood sorrel is found from Nova Scotia and Newfoundland to central New England, as far west as Wisconsin, and in mountains south to North Carolina. It is a plant of rich, moist woodlands. It prefers cool climates, so in the southern part of its range it is found only on mountains.

When it flowers, from May to July, each flower is produced on a separate stalk. The flowers have five notched white petals. Late in the flowering season, more flowers are produced on curved stems at the base of the plant. These flowers never open but self-pollination takes place within the unopened bud, a phenomenon that is called cleistogamy. This unusual method of pollination occurs in a number of other flowers, such as some species of violets.

Dyer's Greenweed

Genista tinctoria L.

Family: *Fabaceae*
Pea family

Additional names:
base broom, dyer's broom, greenweed, greenwood, wood waxen, woud-wix

Dyer's greenweed is a member of the pea family and resembles alfalfa in its explosive pealike flowers, but it is not good for pastures. When cows eat greenweed, their milk has an unpleasant, bitter taste that is retained in butter or cheese.

The name *Genista* is derived from the French word *genet*. The Plantagenet kings of England took their name from their custom of wearing a sprig of greenweed as an emblem. The species name *tinctoria* was given because this plant yields an excellent yellow dye. This species is native to the Mediterranean region and Asia, but it has become established in the eastern United States, in meadows, pastures, and other open places.

The flowers are the typical pea type, with a standard and a keel. The style and the tube of stamens are enclosed in the keel, which is seamed at the top and bottom. The stamens shed their pollen at the top of the keel away from the stigma, so that self-fertilization does not take place. When the flower opens, the stamen tube is under tension on the lower side, which tends to curve it into the top of the keel. When an insect alights on the wing petals of the flower and presses them down, the upper seam of the keel breaks open and the tension causes an explosion. The style is exserted against the pollen-covered underside of the insect. The same explosion causes a shower of pollen, which redusts the insect before it flies to another flower.

The greenweed has been used as a dye since earliest times. It was known as such to the Romans. Dyer's greenweed is mentioned frequently in early literature and was an item of commerce between England and Ireland in the reign of Edward III in 1367. The old English guilds around Winchester used this plant to dye woolen fabrics in about 1400. All parts of the plant can be used for the yellow dye, and when mixed with the blue dye woad, it yields a fine green dye. It has been introduced around the world because of its dyeing properties.

The flowers and the seeds have also been used medicinally to produce diuretic, cathartic, and emetic treatments. The powdered seeds have a purgative action, a fact that was mentioned by Dioscorides and Pliny.

Sheep Laurel

Kalmia angustifolia L.

Family: *Ericaceae*
Heath family

Additional names:
dwarf laurel, lambkill, sheep poison, spoon wood, wichy

This second species of *Kalmia* is a much smaller plant than the mountain laurel. It seldom reaches three feet in height. It is found on upland slopes and hilly pastures in open habitats. As the name *angustifolia* (narrow leaved) would imply, this species has smaller, narrower leaves than mountain laurel. The flowers are also smaller and shallower, and the corolla is a dark pink with a star design outlined in darker red.

As the names *lambkill* and *sheep poison* demonstrate, sheep laurel is as toxic as mountain laurel. It contains a glucoside and a toxic substance called andromedotoxin, present in mountain laurel, too. Since sheep laurel occurs in open places and pastures, grazing sheep may come into contact with it, eat the leaves, and become poisoned.

In spite of its toxic nature, sheep laurel was valued as a medicinal plant by many Indian tribes, mostly for treating skin diseases.

The *Kalmias* have an unusual flower structure. The anthers of the stamens are tucked into pouches in the corolla. The stamens pop out when an insect visits the flower, and the insect is dusted liberally with pollen.

94

Common Milkweed

***Asclepias syriaca**
L.*

Family: *Asclepiadaceae*
Milkweed family

Additional names:
*silky sallow wart,
Virginia silk, wild
asparagus, wild cotton*

Common milkweed is a perennial herb that crops up in every waste place imaginable. It occurs from New Brunswick to Georgia and west to the Mississippi River in abandoned pastures, on roadsides, or even in unweeded city sidewalks.

It is an attractive plant because of its clusters of purplish pink flowers, which begin in June and continue to August. Its single stem differentiates it from the less common showy milkweed *(Asclepias speciosa).*

The milkweeds are so called because they contain a sticky, milky sap, or latex, that protects them from attack by many leaf-eating insects. The sticky sap contains cardiac glycosides known as cardenolides. One insect, however, has coevolved with the milkweeds and feeds on the common milkweed and showy milkweed with impunity. The caterpillars of the monarch butterfly not only feed on the milkweeds but also absorb the poison into their bodies. The poison is passed on to the butterflies, making them bitter and unpalatable to birds. Studies of the winter colonies of monarch butterflies in Mexico show that birds such as the black-backed orioles catch butterflies indiscriminately but eat only those that have less cardenolides in their bodies. The amount of poison in a particular butterfly depends on the poison content of the species of the plant on which the caterpillar fed.

There are many uses for this weedy plant. Those of the silky fruit are described later in this book. Since the mature plant contains potent compounds, it has been useful in folk medicine for the treatment of asthma, coughs, and typhus fever. It has also been used as a contraceptive.

The young shoots are not poisonous and have often been used like asparagus. The common milkweed has also been used as a potherb. The young shoots, unopened buds, and young pods are edible if they are boiled several times in fresh water to remove the poisons. The flowers produce abundant nectar, and some Indians would shake the morning dew from the flowers into a bowl and use it as a sweetener. The French and eastern Canadians adapted this technique to make sugar from the flowers.

Wild Yellow Lily

Lilium canadense L.

Family: *Liliaceae*
Lily family

Additional names:
Canada lily, meadow lily

The wild yellow lily is one of the most common and most widely distributed of all the lilies of North America. It occurs over an area ranging from Nova Scotia and Ontario south down the mountain chains to Georgia and Alabama. It is found westward to Minnesota and Nebraska. This beautiful plant is a species of damp meadows, woodland borders, and fields.

The erect stem bears a number of hanging, yellow-to-orange-red bells that swing in the wind. The flowers tend to be yellow when they first open and to redden with age, but some plants have red flowers from the beginning. The throats of these bells are dotted brown. This species has been introduced into cultivation in part because the mixed yellow and red flowers add a pleasing color to flower borders in June and July.

The bulb of this lily was used by the Algonquins to treat stomach problems, and the Cherokee used boiled bulbs to fatten their children.

This species is closely related to the Michigan lily *(L. michiganense),* but the flowers of that species do not remain bell shaped as the sepals and petals curve over backward to touch the basal tube.

Alfalfa

Medicago sativa L.

Family: *Fabaceae*
Pea family

Additional name:
lucerne

This species came from the Iranian region and has been introduced into Europe and North America because it is an excellent source of cattle fodder. Like various other members of the pea family, it contains nodules of nitrogen-fixing bacteria on the roots.

Alfalfa is one of three main sources for the commercial extraction of carotene, a vitamin A product that is used to enrich baby foods and bird foods. Alfalfa sprouts are one of the most popular bean sprouts because of their high protein content.

The purple flowers have the typical pea flower with a showy upper petal, or standard, and the fused, boat-shaped lower petals, or keel. The flower has an explosive mechanism that projects the stamens and dust pollen onto the abdomen of a landing bee. In this way the plants are fertilized and their small, beanlike pods form from the flowers.

Alfalfa serves a dual purpose: it enriches the soil and so avoids costly fertilization with nitrates, and it is also a valuable fodder crop. It is so valuable to cattle farmers that they often refer to it as "the green gold of forage crops." Its value comes from the fact that when nitrogen is readily available, a plant produces more protein. Alfalfa is protein rich and palatable to cattle, so it is used for hay, silage, and grazing.

Daisy Fleabane

Erigeron strigosus Muhl. ex Willd.

Family: *Asteraceae*
Aster family

Additional name:
white top

The fleabanes are common weeds throughout North America, and this species is no exception. It is a field weed that occurs over most of Canada and the United States.

The name *fleabane* comes from the insecticidal properties of some species of the genus, a common feature of many members of the aster family, the source of the insecticide pyrethrum. The name *Erigeron* comes from the Greek words *eri* (early) and *geron* (an old man), referring to the species' flowering time, which is early in comparison to many other asters.

This particular species is distinguished from the annual daisy fleabane *(Erigeron annuus)* by its lower height (one to two feet) and the hairs on the middle part of the stem, which vary from long and spreading in one variety to short and pressed against the stem. In the other species these hairs are always long and spreading.

The daisy fleabane and other species of fleabane have been used as medicinal plants. For example, some southeastern Indians used a decoction of the roots to relieve pain in their legs after walking too far. The Ojibwe used it to make a cure for headaches. The commonest use is of the oil of erigeron as a styptic to stop external and internal bleeding.

Tall Buttercup

**_Ranunculus acris_
L.**

Family: _Ranunculaceae
Buttercup family_

Additional names:
_butter-rose, common
buttercup, cuckoo-bud,
horse gold, yellow gowan_

This is the most common of all the European buttercup species. It makes many an English meadow a sea of glowing yellow, so it is not surprising that the colonists missed this familiar plant and introduced it to their new American homeland. Now it is found in fields, meadows, roadsides, neglected lawns, and gardens from Nova Scotia to Georgia and in northern states to the West Coast.

One reason for its abundance in meadows is that cattle will leave it uneaten unless they are desperately hungry. This fact was observed by Linnaeus in the meadows of Sweden, where he found that sheep and goats eat this species, but cattle, horses, and pigs refuse it. It causes sores and blisters in the mouths of cows. This led Linnaeus to give this species the name _acris_ or _bitter buttercup._ However, farmers also know that hay containing buttercups is harmless to cattle. The bitter taste is mainly a volatile, oillike substance called protoanemonin. When buttercup plants are made into hay the protoanemonin evaporates, and the plant is no longer acrid or harmful. The chemical is also antibiotic.

The petals of this and other species of buttercups are a particularly bright, waxy, shiny yellow. This is due to the reflection from a special layer of cells just beneath the surface of the petals. The base of the petals are interesting too because of their conspicuous honey glands. Pull off a petal and observe this scalelike gland that produces the nectar to feed the pollinating bees.

Oxeye Daisy

**_Chrysanthemum
leucanthemum
L._**

Family: _Asteraceae
Aster family_

Additional names:
_Dan daisy, Marguerite,
maudlin daisy, white
weed_

This most popular and common wild daisy is another European introduction to North America. The English name _daisy_ is derived from "day's eye." In France, however, this plant is called _Marguerite,_ in honor of the English Queen Margaret of Anjou, who came from France and used the daisy in her coat of arms. This daisy is a relative of mums, or chrysanthemums, a Greek word meaning yellow (chrisos) flower (anthos). The oxeye daisy is yellow and white, but another European species, the corn marigold _(C. segetum),_ has all yellow flowers.

This flower demonstrates clearly the construction of a daisy flower head. We call it a flower, but it is actually a closely united cluster of flowers. This composite flower led to the daisy family's older Latin name, _Compositae,_ but following the recommendations of the Code of Botanical Nomenclature we now call the family _Asteraceae,_ after a genus in the family. The flowers' outer rings have white petals and are called ray flowers. In the oxeye daisy, the ray flowers are all female. The inner yellow flowers are called the disc flowers and can be either male or female.

The oxeye daisy has been used to make an antispasmodic, a diuretic, and a tonic. It has a similar effect as the more popularly used chamomile.

While this plant decorates roadsides, waste places, meadows, and pastures, farmers often dislike it because it gives an unpleasant taste to the milk of cattle that graze on it.

Perhaps the most familiar use of the daisy flower is to discern love by plucking off the ray petals one by one and alternating between "he loves me, he loves me not" until the last petal is gone and the true feelings of the beloved are revealed. If you try this, remember that over ninety percent of the flowers of oxeye daisy have an uneven number of petals, so the odds are nine to one that you will end with the same phrase with which you began the count.

Wild Lupine

Lupinus perennis L.

Family: *Fabaceae Pea family*

Additional names: *blue bean, quaker bonnet*

Lupines have long been a favorite garden flower, and their popularity has increased since George Russell, an amateur gardener from Yorkshire, England, began producing hybrids between the two American species *L. polyphyllus* and *L. arboreus,* which are now known as the Russell hybrid lupines. The wild lupine of the eastern United States and Canada is a member of a large genus of plants that occurs in Europe and in the Americas. There are many species in the western United States and south into the Andes of South America.

The name of the genus could give a false impression of this useful, soil-enriching plant. The Romans named it for the wolf *(lupus)* because they believed that the plant destroyed the fertility of the soil, ravaging it like a wolf. In fact this could not be further from the truth because the lupine is a member of the legume, or pea, family and has root nodules that contain nitrogen-fixing bacteria. Lupines can grow in very poor soil by virtue of their ability to fix their own nitrogen.

Wild lupine grows in fields, on sandy roadsides, and in open woods from Nova Scotia south to Florida and west to Louisiana and Minnesota. At times its profusion turns Midwestern hayfields blue with lupine flowers in early summer. Since the lupine is advantageous to the pastures because of its nitrogen-fixing ability, it is a useful source of green fodder. The flowers are usually bluish purple but can occasionally be pink or even, rarely, white.

Perhaps the best-known lupine in North America is the Texas bluebonnet. It is a low-growing, prairie lupine *(Lupinus subcarnosus)* that decorates the spring roadsides in Texas and is the Texas state flower.

105

Purple Fringed Orchid

Platanthera grandiflora (Bigelow) Lindley

Family: *Orchidaceae Orchid family*

Additional names: *greater purple fringed orchid, large butterfly orchid, large purple fringed orchid*

In contrast to the inconspicuous ragged fringed orchid, the purple fringed orchid is the most attractive of all the orchid species found in the northeast. It is a plant of moist woodland, swamp margins, and damp meadows, and it often occurs in great abundance. This species is found from Newfoundland to West Virginia and further south to North Carolina in mountainous areas. It grows as far west as Wisconsin and Tennessee.

The large lavender-to-purple flowers are dramatic because of its three-lobed, fringed lip and the large, backward-pointing spur that is almost an inch in length. The flowers are visited and pollinated by butterflies and moths. The tiger swallowtail butterfly and the small gray moth were found by botanist Carl Stoutamire to be pollinators of this species.

In the fringed orchids the pollinia, or pollen masses, have sticky areas, or viscidia, that catch onto the moth's or butterfly's tongue as it probes the spur to gather the nectar. A pollinium is then carried on the insect's tongue to another flower. When the insect inserts its tongue into the new flower, the pollinium is placed on the stigma and pollination is effected.

The large purple fringed orchid is very closely related to another species, the small purple fringed orchid *(Platanthera psycodes),* which grows in similar habitats. The differences between the two species are in size and in the column structure. The small fringed orchid has a small dumbbell-shaped opening to the spur and a smaller, narrower column than the greater fringed orchid.

Common St. Johnswort

Hypericum perforatum L.

Family: *Hypericaceae*
St. Johnswort family

Additional names: *goatweed, goldenwood, klamathweed*

Although this is an introduced European plant, it is now the most common St. Johnswort in North America. It is found from Newfoundland to Florida and throughout Canada and the United States. It is a weed of meadows and roadsides. It was either accidentally introduced with grain seed or brought over because of its use in folk medicine and witchcraft. It begins to produce its bright yellow flowers around June twenty-fourth, or St. John's Eve. It was gathered and hung on doors and windows in medieval England to ward off evil spirits and thunder. Probably no other plant has as many superstitions attached to it as the common St. Johnswort. One superstition was that the dew that fell on this plant on St. John's Eve was a most effective preventative of eye disease.

The yellow petals have black dots on their margins. The stemless leaves, which are attached directly to the stem, have black dots scattered over their surface. If the leaf is held against the light these dots, which are oil glands, become transparent.

Although St. Johnswort is an attractive plant and a relative of the commonly cultivated rose of Sharon, it is abhorred by most farmers. It spreads rapidly with its creeping stem and is poisonous to cattle. The glandular dots on the leaves contain a quinone called hypericine, which causes photosensitization in white-skinned cows. Its effect can be so strong that the animals become demented by the intensity of the itching and rub the affected areas of skin until it hangs off in strips.

The leaves have also been used in folk medicine as an astringent, aromatic, expectorant, and nervine. It was held effective for many other ailments such as jaundice and diarrhea. An ointment made from the flowers of St. Johnswort was called "balm-of-the-warrior's-wound."

Harebell

Campanula rotundifolia L.

Family: *Campanulaceae*
Bellflower family

Additional name: *bluebell of Scotland*

thou shalt not lack
The flower that's like thy face, pale primrose, nor
The azur'd hare-bell, like thy veins.
Cymbeline, *IV.ii.220–222*

The members of the bellflower genus are called *Campanula*. This name is derived from the diminutive of the Latin *campana,* meaning a bell. "Little bell" is an appropriate name for the harebell, the most dainty of our bellflowers, with its small, nodding bell-shaped flowers borne on threadlike, almost invisible, stalks. Although the species name is *rotundifolia,* or round leaves, you have probably observed that the leaves on the stem are narrow and lanceolate. Only the basal leaves, which occur in spring when the plant first emerges, are round. It must have been those leaves that were the reason for the name.

This is a widespread species in both Europe and North America. It grows from Northern Canada south to West Virginia and Texas. It extends to the West Coast and north to Oregon. It grows in open places, in meadows, on grassy slopes, roadsides, shores, and rocky banks.

Unlike many of the more robust bellflowers, the harebell is hard to cultivate. It often dies out when planted in gardens, but if it does get established in partially shaded, moist places, it makes an elegant rock garden plant.

109

Deptford Pink

Dianthus armeria L.

Family: *Caryophyllaceae Carnation family*

This plant originated in Europe. It is a wild relative of the carnation and the sweet William and has naturalized widely in North America from Nova Scotia and Ontario south to Georgia. The genus was officially named *Dianthus* by Linnaeus. However, he used an older name from the work of French botanist Caspar Bauhin, who was born in 1550 and who recognized ten species of pinks in his 1596 book *Pinax Theatri Botanici.*

It is hardly surprising that the attractive Deptford pink, with its deep rose-red colored, sweetly scented flowers, was introduced to North America in colonial times. The ragged edges of the petals enhance the beauty of this plant. It can be found along roadsides and in dry fields.

The common name comes from the town of Deptford, in England. Today Deptford is part of the urban area of London, but formerly it must have once been known for its abundance of pinks.

English Plantain

Plantago lanceolata L.

Family: *Plantaginaceae Plantain family*

Additional names: *black jack, black plantain, buckthorn plantain, cocks hen plant, lamb's tongue, long plantain, narrow-leaved plantain, rib-grass, ribwort, ripple grass, snake plantain*

This pestilent weed from England and Europe must have been brought to America accidentally. Like many other weeds, it is easily dispersed and probably came as a stow-away with some more desirable species. The English plantain is now a weed of lawns, fields, and waste places throughout North America.

It has a wide distribution because the seeds have an unusual mucilaginous coating. This ensures that when they are damp they adhere to anything with which they come in contact. These seeds are found so often as "strays" in commercial packs of grass seeds that many places have noxious weed laws restricting the amount of impure or stray seeds that are permitted. For example, in Oregon not more than 360 plantain seeds per pound of crop seed, such as clover or grass, are allowed.

In England, plantain is usually called *ribwort,* or by some other name that refers to the three to five prominent, parallel leaf-veins that make this plant look more like a grass than a dicotyledonous species. The flowers are produced in tight clusters that open from the bottom upward. Plantain is popular with English children, who call it "soldiers and sailors" and play a game with the flower heads. One person holds the flower stalk out horizontally and the opponent uses another one to try to knock the flower head off. The game continues until one flower stalk is decapitated.

Although we tend to think only evil of this plant, some farmers like it because the mucilaginous leaves make excellent sheep fodder. It grows on poor land where nothing else will grow and so puts land that would otherwise be waste land to a productive use. The mucilage around the seed coat was used in France for stiffening muslin and other fabrics. The seeds are also a favorite food of many birds and are in some bird seed mixtures. All this proves that what is a weed to some people is a useful plant to others.

Blue Flag

Iris versicolor L.

Family: *Iridaceae*
Iris family

Additional names:
flag lily, fleur-de-luce, water flag, wild iris

The blue flag, or flower-de-luce, has been described in lyrical detail by Henry Wadsworth Longfellow in his poem "Flower-de-luce."

> *Beautiful Lily, dwelling by still rivers,*
> *Or solitary mere,*
> *Or where the sluggish meadow-brook delivers*
> *Its waters to the weir!*
>
> *Thou laughest at the mill, the whir and worry*
> *Of spindle and of loom,*
> *And the great wheel that toils amid the hurry*
> *And rushing of the flume.*
>
> *Born to the purple, born to joy and pleasance,*
> *Thou dost not toil nor spin,*
> *But makest glad and radiant with thy presence*
> *The meadow and the lin.*
>
> *The wind blows and uplifts thy drooping banner,*
> *And round thee throng and run*
> *The rushes, the green yeomen of thy manor,*
> *The outlaws of the sun.*

The blue flag is one of the most beautiful of all North American swamp plants. It is common in marshes, swamps, and wet shores from Nova Scotia to Virginia. The genus name *Iris* is Greek for rainbow, and this species has the name *versicolor,* or many colors. The flowers of blue flag do not have all the colors of the rainbow, but the flowers sport many hues on the darkly veined violet and blue petals, which contrast with the bright yellow petallike sepals. The three upper parts of the flower are the sepals, which are turned downward over the other floral parts. Insects that are attracted by the sepals must crawl under them and in so doing touch one of the styles and stamens and effect pollination.

The thick, creeping rhizomes of the blue flag are quite poisonous but have also been used in folk medicine to make a powerful carthartic. The Chippewa and Potawatomi Indians applied the root to external swellings and bruises. The roots have also been used as a diuretic and to eliminate worms. The blue flag roots possess the ability to increase the rate of fat catabolism and have been used in India for the treatment of obesity. However, this is a plant to avoid consuming in any way because of the iridin poisons it contains. The roots are a source for commercial iridin.

The Indians put the poison to use. They mixed it with animal bile and put the mixture into a buffalo's gall bladder, which was then hung to warm for several days near a fire. Arrow tips were dipped into the mixture and then used to cause the quick death of their enemies. It took a few days for those who were only slightly wounded to die.

The leaves of blue flag were also used as a source of a green dye by the Indians of Quebec.

113

Japanese Honeysuckle

Lonicera japonica Thunb.

Family: *Caprifoliaceae Honeysuckle family*

Although this popular plant is a native of Asia and was introduced to America from China in 1806, during the last 150 years it has escaped from cultivation and become a common plant from New England south to Florida and west to Kansas and Texas. It is now abundant in woodlands, on roadsides, and in thickets and competes so well with the native flora that it is often a pest. This fast-growing vine can smother trees and take over large areas of woodland. It has become part of the landscape especially along riversides and roads. It was imported because it has attractive, profuse flowers with a sweet scent, but most foresters wish that it had never been imported! On the other hand, gardeners love this evergreen vine because it grows so vigorously and soon climbs up trellises or hides ugly fences and garden sheds.

Honeysuckle has long been a popular flower, and the European species is mentioned several times by William Shakespeare. Since it is a true plant of midsummer, it is not surprising that the doting Queen Titania murmured to the bewitched Bottom, the weaver:

> *Sleep thou, and I will wind thee in my arms.*
> *Fairies, be gone, and be all ways away.*
> *So doth the woodbine the sweet honeysuckle*
> *Gently entwist.*
> A Midsummer Night's Dream, *IV.i.39–42*

The fragrant flowers are white when they first open and become a creamy yellow as they age. Their trumpet-shaped petals lure hummingbirds and insects in the day and hawkmoths at night. The flowers produce abundant nectar to feed the pollinators. Even children enjoy pinching off the green receptacle at the base of the flower and carefully grasping the bottom of the pistil between the thumb and forefinger, then slowly pulling it down through the petal tube, until it emerges with a drop of tasty nectar. This nectar is used as a medicine and as a soft-drink ingredient in China.

The flowers open in the evening, and the anthers have opened slowly before releasing the pollen. At this time the style projects beyond the anther, and the flower moves into the horizontal position. At first the style is bent downward and the stamens form a platform on which the insects alight and are dusted with pollen. Later, by the second day, the style moves up into a horizontal position and the stamens shrivel and bend down. At that time the insects will come into contact with the style. The pollen from another plant will be left on the style by the insect, so the flower is cross-fertilized.

115

Purple Flowering Raspberry

Rubus odoratus L.

Family: *Rosaceae*
Rose family

Additional names:
flowering raspberry,
Virginia raspberry

This rather thin and straggling shrub is a widespread species found in thickets and rocky woodlands from Ontario and Nova Scotia south to Georgia and Tennessee. It grows to five feet tall and puts up numerous, erect canes. Unlike most other members of the genus *Rubus,* which includes the blackberries and raspberries, the branches are thornless. The young branches, however, are very sticky because they are covered with a clammy type of hair.

The five-lobed leaves are reminiscent of a maple leaf. This species is quite closely related to the thimbleberry *(Rubus parviflorus),* which has smaller leaves and white flowers. The large, attractive rose-purple flowers are produced all summer long. This means that fruit ripen over an extended period, from summer into early fall. They are edible but not flavorful when compared with the cultivated raspberry, which is another species of *Rubus.*

The soft, hairy leaves were used by the Indians of Quebec to line the inside of their leather shoes.

117

Greater Bladderwort

Utricularia vulgaris L.

Family:
Lentibulariaceae
Bladderwort family

This small, floating, yellow-flowered aquatic plant is another carnivorous plant. Unlike the sundew, which has a passive trapping mechanism, the bladderworts have an active and effective trap. The underwater branches of this plant are covered with a large number of minute, inflated bladders. These small pouches have a hinge door at one end, to which a few bristles are attached. When the bristles are touched by a small animal, they trigger the trap by lifting the door. This means that water rushes into the bladder and sucks the helpless prey inside. Once the prey is trapped, the plant begins to digest the animal and then resets itself to capture something else. It may be a water flea, a tiny crustacean, an insect larva, or any other hapless, small animal that bumps into the trigger hairs.

The bladderwort has no roots since it does not need them either to anchor the plant in the ground or to absorb nutrients. The flowering stem emerges from below the water and bears attractive yellow flowers. The bladderwort also forms winter buds. These rest on the pond bottom and over winter. It reproduces both by these vegetative buds and by seed dispersal.

There are fifteen species of bladderwort in the eastern United States. Most of these have yellow flowers, but two species produce purple ones. Worldwide there are 250 species of bladderwort, which are widely distributed in both temperate and tropical regions wherever there are suitable bogs, lakes, and ponds for their unusual life-style.

Round-leaved Sundew

Drosera rotundifolia L.

Family: *Droseraceae*
Sundew family

Additional names:
common sundew, eyebright, lustwort, moor grass, youth wort

The famous scientist and formulator of the theory of evolution, Charles Darwin, wrote:

During the summer of 1860, I was surprised by finding how large a number of insects are caught by the leaves of the common sundew (Drosera rotundifolia). I had heard that insects were thus caught but knew nothing further on the subject. I gathered by chance a dozen plants bearing fifty-six fully expanded leaves, and on thirty-one of these dead insects . . . adhered.

This aroused Darwin's curiosity about insectivorous plants and eventually led him to write his book *Insectivorous Plants*. It was published in 1886 and was the pioneering treatise on the subject.

The sundews are one of several types of plants that catch insects to supplement their nutrition. Others include the pitcher plants and the Venus's-flytrap. Insectivorous plants mostly grow in acid bogs where little nitrogen is available. They are able to obtain nitrogen from the nitrogen-rich chitin that makes up the shell of insects. The sundews capture insects with sticky, glandular hairs on the leaves. Insects are attracted to the glistening red leaves, and when they alight on them they are stuck. Immediately the hairs begin to move and envelop the insect. The plant begins to secrete enzymes to digest the insects so that the nutrients can be absorbed through the leaves.

The sundew and other insectivorous plants are attractive and get attention, so they are often cultivated. However, unless good bog conditions are created, they will die. Some insectivorous plants are threatened with extinction because collectors have ravished the wild populations. Do not buy a sundew, a pitcher plant, or a Venus's-flytrap unless you are sure it has been grown from seed rather than dug up from the wild. This will ensure that we may all continue to enjoy these plants and preserve them for future generations.

Brown-rayed Knapweed

Centaurea jacea
L.

Family: *Asteraceae*
Aster family

Additional names:
brown radiant knapweed, knapwort harshweed

The famous seventeenth-century herbalist Culpeper wrote that knapweed is "helpful against coughs, asthma, and difficulty of breathing and good for diseases of the head or nerves. . . . Outwardly the bruised herb is famous for taking away black and blue marks out of the skin."

It is a European and Asian species that has become naturalized in many places in North America. On this continent, it is a plant of roadsides, fields, and waste places. It has thistlelike flowers, but the bracts, unlike those of thistles, are spineless. Several European species of knapweeds are now common in North America. This species is related to the spotted knapweed *(Centaurea maculosa)* but differs in that the leaves are less deeply lobed. There are more than four hundred species of knapweed, and even at the time when Linnaeus began botanical nomenclature in 1753, he placed fifty species in his genus *Centaurea*.

Pokeweed

***Phytolacca
americana
L.***

Family: *Phytolaccaceae
Pokeweed family*

Additional names:
*American nightshade,
American spinach, bear's
grape, cancer root,
coakum, inkberry,
pokeberry, pokeroot,
poke salad, skoke,
Virginian poke*

This purple-stemmed shrublike herb helps and hinders mankind. It has many uses, but is also the source of much distress, by poisoning. It is a roadside weed that grows from Quebec and Ontario south to Mexico. It also grows in damp places and open woods. The stem is produced annually from a thick and fleshy perennial root. As the stem matures, it turns purple, giving the plant a striking appearance, especially when the dark purple fruit are mature.

The young shoots are often used as greens. They can be eaten only before the shoots have turned red, and the water in which they are boiled must be changed several times to remove poisons and the bitter taste. The most poisonous part of the plant is the roots. Although the berries have been used to add color to port wines in Portugal, they also are poisonous and should never be eaten. The berries have often been used as a dye for wool and cotton and as a source of ink by the Pennsylvania Dutch.

There are many medicinal uses for pokeweed. An ointment made from the roots has often been used to treat skin diseases, and it is important as a slow emetic and as a purgative. However, the purgative effect of this species is nothing compared with that of the appropriately named *Phytolacca drastica* of Chile!

Many Indian groups used pokeweed in their medicine. The Cherokee used the root tea for treatment of eczema and kidney ailments, a wine from the berry for rheumatism, and a poultice from the berry for cancer, sores, and swellings. The Rappahannock steeped the roots in brine to treat poison ivy.

Recent medical research by G. J. Teltow and other researchers of Southwest Texas State University have found an antiviral agent in pokeweed that inhibits the multiplication of the herpes viruses. Pokeweed has also been found to have molluscicidal properties. It could possibly be used for controlling fresh-water snails that carry the tropical parasitic disease bilharzia, which plagues areas of Africa and South America.

Pokeweed is a most useful and beautiful plant, but it is also toxic.

Wood Lily

Lilium philadelphicum L.

Family: *Liliaceae*
Lily family

This beautiful, showy lily is widespread in the woodlands of Canada and south to West Virginia, and along the mountain ranges to North Carolina and Kentucky.

The stems grow out of an underground bulb and bear the leaves in whorls. Above the uppermost leaf whorl, the flowers open. The petals are orange-red, with purplish brown spots that mark the paths to the nectar for the insects.

The bulb has been used by Indians in many ways. The Dakota chewed or pulverized the flowers to make an application to cure spider bites. The Malecite used it for the treatment of bruises, cough, fever, and swelling. It was used for poultices to place on sores by the Menominee. The bulbs were also used as an emergency food by many Indian groups, but we should not eat them because this endangers the species. The plant appears to be palatable and to have few defenses against predators; thus only a few plants reach the flowering stage. Deer browse heavily on the plant, and mice enjoy the bulb.

I do not count the hours I spend working. The feeling of timelessness gives me the freedom and peace I need for my work. Not only does this work bring me closer to nature, but it also establishes a bond with history. The painters of the sixteenth and seventeenth centuries are no strangers. When I look at their flower paintings, I lose the feeling of the centuries that separate us.

125

Daylily

Hemerocallis fulva L.

Family: *Liliaceae*
Lily family

Additional names: *fulvous daylily, orange tawny daylily*

This beautiful and popular plant seems typically American because it grows profusely in meadows, by roadsides, and in gardens. However, it is actually a native of eastern Asia that was introduced by the colonists. Together with its smaller relative the yellow daylily (*H. flava*), it has become part of the American scene.

The orange-flowered daylily is apparently a hybrid plant because it does not produce fertile seeds. It reproduces itself vegetatively from the roots. Today there are hundreds of varieties of daylilies available, and this is mainly due to one person, A. B. Stout, who worked for most of his career at The New York Botanical Garden. He collected and hybridized many species of *Hemerocallis* to produce the variety of colors that we have today. In 1934 Dr. Stout wrote the classic book on daylilies (*Daylilies: The Wild Species and Garden Clones, Both Old and New, of the Genus* Hemerocallis), which is still being reprinted today.

The daylily is not only a horticultural delight, it is useful because the entire plant is edible. Flower buds fried in butter taste like green beans. The flowers themselves are considered a great delicacy in China, where they are used fresh or dried. Half-kilo packages of daylily flowers are a common feature in Chinese shops. They are called *gum-tsoy,* or golden vegetable, and are eaten in soups and with noodles. These dried flowers are also used in Chinese medicine.

Hedge Bindweed

Convolvulus sepium L.

Family: *Convolvulaceae*
Morning glory family

Additional names:
bearbind, greater bindweed, hedge convolvulus, old man's night cap

This long, trailing vine is an aggressive weed that is hard to eradicate. The bindweeds belong to the genus *Convolvulus,* the name of which is derived from the Latin *convolvulere,* to twine. Twining is exactly what the plant does, often in places where it is a nuisance such as in gardens or pastures. Many climbing plants twine in a particular direction. The hedge bindweed will always twine from right to left, contrary to the direction of the sun.

This species is found from Newfoundland south to North Carolina and across the United States. It is also a native of Europe, where it is known as hedge bindweed because of its propensity for climbing over and often smothering the hedgerows of Britain. The Latin name *sepium* is derived from *sepes,* meaning a hedge.

Like most other bindweeds, this plant possesses purgative properties. The roots were used in European folk medicine for their carthartic properties.

The hedge bindweed is a serious pest because of its persistent growth. It is hard to eradicate from an area because a small portion of root remaining in the soil will soon produce a shoot with new leaves and a new twining stem. Farmers in some areas where bindweed is a problem have devised many methods to destroy this plant varying from frequent cutting to weaken the rootstock, to using pigs in the pasture because they like to eat the roots, to using chemicals. Some farmers regard this plant as the most noxious of all weeds in spite of its attractive, trumpet-shaped pink or white flowers.

Indian Cucumber Root

Medeola
virginiana
L.

Family: *Liliaceae*
Lily family

The delicate, green flowers of this member of the lily family are borne at the top of the stem above two whorls of leaves. The upper whorl has three small leaves that are one to three inches long, and the lower whorl has six to ten large leaves, up to five inches in length. It is found from Quebec and Nova Scotia south to Florida and west to Alabama. It bears its flowers in early summer, but it is also particularly attractive in the fall, when the leaves turn red and the berries ripen to dark purple.

The genus was named after Medea, the sorceress who was described by Ovid. The white root, about three inches long and up to one inch in diameter, tastes and smells like a cucumber. Indians are reputed to have used it for food. The root was also used as a diuretic by some of the eastern woodland Indian tribes.

This plant has an intricate timing mechanism to ensure it will be pollinated. The six stamens of this species are arranged in two separate rings. The three stamens of the first ring release their pollen early. This is before the stigmas are ready to receive pollen, and so it is carried to other flowers and effects cross-pollination. The second ring opens later, after the stigmas have been receptive to pollen for some time. If they have not been cross-pollinated, they can be self-fertilized from the pollen of the second whorl.

Spotted Jewelweed

Impatiens
capensis
Meerb.

Family: *Balsaminaceae*
Touch-me-not family

Additional names:
quick-in-the-hand,
snapweed, spotted
balsam, spotted
touch-me-not

This is a succulent annual plant that grows in shaded wetlands and pastures from Newfoundland to Georgia and west to Oklahoma and Missouri. The fleshy stems are almost translucent, and the leaves repel water like a duck's back. As a result, beads of dew that form on the leaves sparkle like jewels when the early morning sun strikes them.

The yellow-to-orange-red flowers are mottled. They have three petals, and a petallike sepal that forms a spur, which is full of nectar. Long-tongued bees, butterflies, and hummingbirds are the only creatures that can reach the nectar at the base of the spur.

In addition to its attractive orange flowers, this plant also produces small, inconspicuous green cleistogamous flowers that never open to allow pollination. Instead they are self-pollinated, a process that occurs in many species of violets. However, each large, colored flower encourages cross-fertilization by functioning first as a male and later as a female, a process called protandry. When they open as male flowers, the sticky pollen is deposited on any visitor. For their female role, the anthers drop off and the stigma becomes receptive to pollen so that later bird or insect visitors will deposit rather than receive pollen.

Many of the names given to this plant refer to the mature fruit's habit of exploding. Many children (and adults) have had fun helping the dispersal of jewelweeds by touching the ripe fruit and watching the seeds shoot out away from the parent plant. The outer layer of the fruit capsules is turgid, and this puts a strain on the whole fruit. A light touch causes the valves to roll violently upward and inward and to scatter the seeds in all directions.

The jewelweeds are used as spring greens. The young shoots are boiled in water, and the water is changed twice. The sap of the stem has been used to treat poison ivy, but it is not an effective remedy. The plant has, however, been shown to be fungicidal, and it is used to treat athlete's foot and other skin fungi.

131

Fragrant Water Lily

**Nymphaea
odorata
Dryand. ex Ait.**

Family: *Nymphaeaceae
Water lily family*

Additional names:
*large white water lily,
sweet-scented water lily,
water nymph, white pond
lily, white water lily*

This is one of the most common of all the white water lilies. It occurs from New-foundland to Florida and west to Texas. The floating leaves and flowers grow from a perennial rootstock, which is anchored at the bottom of a pond or slowly moving stream. The large flowers, which are three to five inches in diameter, are sweet scented and attract pollen-gathering insects. The flowers open at dawn but are closed by noon.

The rhizomes of the fragrant water lily are extremely rich in tannins and so have been used in medicine as an astringent and as a source of a black dye. The Chippewa Indians employed the dried and finely powdered roots for the treatment of mouth sores; other tribes used the roots for treatment of vaginal sores. The Ojibwe also used the powdered roots as a poultice for sores and swellings.

Plants have evolved many adaptations to cope with the different habitats in which they grow. The leaves and stems of this plant are surrounded by a gelatinous substance that serves to waterproof the plant. The leafstalk consists of a spongy material with large air channels inside. This is an adaptation to ensure that the oxygen taken in by leaves is carried to the roots. Another adaptation in the water lily is that the stomata (pores through which gas exchange takes place) are on the upper surface of the leaf rather than on the under surface, as in the majority of plants. If the stomata were submerged they would not be able to function.

A fanciful Indian legend tells of the origin of the water lily. It came from a bright star that appeared in the sky above a village. The star looked down serenely on the happy Indians, but they became perturbed by its presence. At last, after many discussions and consultations, they sent one of their chiefs to the top of the mountain to ask the star what it portended. In awe, the chief listened to the star's explanation that it shone on this happy people, liked what it had seen, and had now decided to live with them. The chief returned with the good news to his people, and soon after the star came down to live on top of the mountain. But the star found it was still too distant from the people, so it moved to the top of the tallest tree in the forest. This was nearer, but the dense foliage obscured the view of the village. The star returned to the sky to think. Finally it resolved to place itself in the lake, and overnight the star came to earth. The next morning the Indians woke up to find a glorious new flower in their lake: the first water lily.

132

Pickerelweed

**Pontederia
cordata
L.**

Family: *Pontederiaceae*
Water hyacinth family

The pickerel fish live in the habitat along the margins of streams and lakes where the water hyacinth is found. This environmental association has led to naming the plant after the pickerel fish.

Pickerelweed is an aquatic plant that grows along the edges of ponds, marshes, and streams from Nova Scotia south to Florida. It is a relative of the water hyacinth, a noxious tropical weed. Pickerelweed grows from a creeping rhizome embedded in the pond. The flower spikes and leaves grow out of it, but unlike the water lily the leaves of pickerelweed are erect rather than prone.

It is attractive because of the blue flower spikes, which produce a few flowers each day over an extended flowering period, from June to October. The petals appear violet-blue from a distance, but a closer examination shows that the upper petal bears a yellow spot, which serves as a nectar guide. It signals bees to enter the flower in search of nectar and so effect pollination.

High Mallow

Malva sylvestris L.

Family: *Malvaceae Mallow family*

Additional names: *blue mallow, cheeses, common mallow*

This is a tall, robust species of mallow from Europe that is common in hedges, fields, and waste places. The showy flowers are usually more purple than those of the more common pink-flowered musk mallow. The fruits are reminiscent of a wheel of cheese, hence the common name *cheeses* given to this and some other species of mallow.

The flowers of mallows, and the related hibiscus, have a special structure in their centers called an androgynophore, which bears the stamens and the stigma. When the flower first opens, the anthers are arranged in a group over the undeveloped and unreceptive stigma. The anthers shed their pollen and then become limp and droop. This makes room for the styles to elongate, and they take the anthers' place. Insects that visit a newly opened flower brush against the stamens and are dusted with pollen. When they fly onto an older flower, they touch the stigmas and dust them with pollen. This timing device in the flower makes self-fertilization unlikely, and the mallow is cross-pollinated.

Many plants have evolved different mechanisms for outbreeding. The ability to cross-pollinate is important for plants to ensure their competitive strength.

Bouncing Bet

Saponaria officinalis L.

Family: *Caryophyllaceae Pink family*

Additional names: *bruisewort, fuller's herb, latherwort, London pride, soaproot, soapwort, sweet Betty, wild sweet William*

This is a southern European member of the pink family. It was quickly introduced to North America by colonists, who grew it in their gardens because of its usefulness. It has naturalized as a common plant of roadsides and disturbed areas throughout the western United States and Canadian provinces.

It is still frequently grown as a garden flower and resembles the more popular phlox. The attractive pink flowers, which are often double, are scented at night, and their color attracts butterflies during the day.

The name *bouncing bet* has an imaginative derivation. It is said to be because the flower suggests the rear view of an old-fashioned washerwoman wearing numerous petticoats and ruffles, bobbing up and down as she scrubs the clothes.

This plant is also frequently called *soapwort* because it is rich in saponins, which produce a lather when mixed with water. It was used as a substitute for soap by the colonists. In summer the leaves and stems were used for washing, and the dried roots were stored for winter use. The saponins foam and dislodge dirt particles from clothing. The roots were used by the English textile industry for the process of preparing, or fulling, the cloth. Soapwort thus became known as *fuller's herb* and was cultivated by the textile industry of New England. It is still used for washing antique textiles and is probably the most widely used soap plant of Europe. And British brewers discovered that the addition of a little soapwort helped to produce a good foamy head on their beer!

Bouncing bet also had many medicinal uses in Europe, especially for the treatment of itches and for serious skin sores caused by syphilis and other veneral diseases. The whole plant is mildly poisonous because of its high content of saponins and should be used only externally.

137

Tufted Vetch

**Vicia cracca
L.**

Family: *Fabaceae
Pea family*

Additional names:
*blue vetch, cow vetch,
fitch, tine grass*

This representative of the many species of vetches in North America is actually a European introduction. It now occurs throughout southern Canada and south to North Carolina and Illinois. It is a most beautiful climbing plant that decorates roadsides and fields throughout the summer. Its pea-type flowers, in shades of lavender to bright blue, can be found from May through August.

The genus name for vetches is derived from the Latin word *vincio* (to bind or twine), and this refers to the climbing, twining nature of this plant. Like many members of the pea family, the tufted vetch has been cultivated in pastures because of its nitrogen-fixing property. The roots contain the bacteria-filled nodules that fix atmospheric nitrogen, which is why the escaped vetches can colonize so well in roadsides and waste places on poor soil.

The vetches and many other climbing plants have tendrils that assist their climbing over hedges and thickets. The compound leaves, each with eight to twelve pairs of leaflets, terminate in an apical pair of leaflets that have become tendrils. At the base of each leaf is a pair of stipules that are shaped like arrowheads. Stipules are a feature of most members of the pea family.

At first, the flowers are pink, but they become blue to violet as they age. They are pollinated by bees. When the bee lands on the tightly interlocked wing and keel petals, they are depressed together, and first the stigma is exposed from within the keel. It brushes off any pollen brought on the bee's body from another flower. After this, the pollen of the flower on which the bee has landed, which has already been shed into the apex of the keel, is brushed out by a tuft of hairs onto the bee. When the bee flies off, the flower springs back to its normal shape.

This is also one of the many plants that have an explosive mechanism of seed dispersal. The small, lanceolate pods are about an inch in length. When the pod is ripe, the unequal contraction of the cells causes a tension, and as it dries further the tension increases until the sides split apart violently, throwing the small, round, black seeds some distance from the parent plant.

Toadflax

Linaria vulgaris Mill

Family:
Scrophulariaceae
Snapdragon family

Additional names:
butter-and-eggs, churnstaff, dragon-bushes, eggs and bacon, eggs and collops, flaxweed, fluellin, monkey flower, pattens and clogs, snapdragon

This attractive European introduction is now as widespread throughout North America as it is on its native continent. It is a common plant in waste places, along roadsides, and in dry, open meadows. It probably reached America as seed in grain and is often regarded as a troublesome weed.

Many of its local names, such as *butter-and-eggs* and *eggs and bacon,* refer to the flowers that have two shades of yellow. The upper lips of the corolla are lemon yellow, and the three-lobed lower lip is an orange, yolklike color. It has a conspicuous nectar spur at the base.

The flower structure is identical to that of the garden snapdragon. Its corolla is tightly closed until it is forced open by a bee. Only large bees with tongues long enough to reach the nectar in the spur are able to force the flowers open. As the bee pushes its way into the throat of the flower and probes with its tongue for nectar, it is dusted with pollen from the stamens, which are borne against the roof of the flower.

The common name *toadflax* arose because the curiously shaped, closed flowers resemble small toads and the mouth of the flower resembles a toad's mouth.

In folk medicine, the toadflax is a well-known remedy for jaundice and liver ailments. This is an easy-to-explain example of the ancient "doctrine of signatures," where like was used to treat like. The yellow flowers would lead logically to its being used for the disease that turns one yellow.

Yarrow

Achillea millefolium L.

Family: *Asteraceae*
Aster family

Additional names:
bloodwort, carpenter's weed, devil's nettle, devil's plaything, dog daisy, milfoil, military herb, nosebleed, old man's pepper, sanguinary, sneezewort, soldier's woundwort, staunchweed, thousand leaf, yarroway

The many names of this plant tell its story. It is said to be the plant that Achilles used to stop the bleeding of his wounded soldiers in the Trojan wars. As a result Romans referred to yarrow as *herba militaris,* and Linnaeus named the genus for Achilles. The names that refer to sneezing and nosebleeds are from the European custom of using the leaf to divine a lover's intent—while tickling the inside of the nostril, a chant was made:

Yarroway, yarroway, bear a white bow,
If my love love me, my nose will bleed now.

If a nosebleed ensued it was a good omen. Yarrow has long been used in magic and divination in many different places. The Chinese used the dried stems of yarrow to divine the future by casting them to form the hexagrams that occur in the *Book of Changes* or *I Ching.* Many other superstitions are attached to yarrow.

Yarrow is an aromatic plant and, apart from its use as a styptic, has been used as a medicine in many ways throughout its natural range. The native American variety has a round-topped inflorescence, while that of Eurasia is flat-tipped. The flowers are generally white, but red, pink, and lilac varieties occur.

Some of the red and pink varieties have been introduced into cultivation. Yarrow belongs to a large genus of plants with over one hundred species, and several of its relatives are common garden plants. The fern leaf yarrow *(Achillea filipendulina)* is the most common cultivated one and has golden yellow flowers. Such varieties as coronation gold and gold plate are popular garden plants.

The wild yarrow occurs widely as a weed in fields and lawns, in meadows, and on shores and sandy slopes over a range that extends to Europe, Asia, and North America from Labrador to Alaska and south to Florida, California, and Mexico.

Black-eyed Susan

Rudbeckia hirta
L.

Family: *Asteraceae*
Aster family

This ubiquitous plant of the fields and prairies of summer, and even of some gardens (as cultivars), has long been a favorite of many people. It is the state flower of Maryland. The source of the name is unclear, for nobody knows who Susan was and the eyes of the plant named after her are brown, not black.

Linnaeus named this North American genus of plants after his botanical predecessors, the Rudbecks of Uppsala, Sweden. The first Rudbeck founded the botanical garden in Uppsala where Linnaeus studied. The older Rudbeck was succeeded as professor of botany by his son, Olaf Rudbeck, who was Linnaeus's teacher. Later Linnaeus succeeded Olaf Rudbeck as professor. With this multiple connection with the Rudbeck family, it is not surprising that the founder of the modern system of biological naming called a genus of plants *Rudbeckia*.

The species of *Rudbeckia* are divided into two groups: the *hirta* group, which includes black-eyed Susan and its relatives, and the *laciniata* group, which includes the green-headed coneflower *(Rudbeckia laciniata)*. The coneflower group is larger than the *hirta* group and includes yellow ray flowers and green-to-greenish-brown disc flowers. The hirta group has the familiar bright yellow ray flowers and dark brown disc flowers of the black-eyed Susan.

The black-eyed Susan species *(R. hirta)* is showy and bright. It has also been much cultivated, and many garden varieties now exist, including the popular Gloriosa Daisy.

The Cherokee Indians used an extract of the roots of black-eyed Susan for the treatment of earache and the dried flowers to make a tea that was used as a tonic.

Chicory

**Cichorium
intybus
L.**

Family: *Asteraceae
Aster family*

Additional names:
*blue daisy, bunk, coffee
weed, succory, wild
succory*

This European and North African plant has become one of the most common weeds along the roadsides, fences, and fields of the northeastern United States and Canada. Although it is often regarded as a weed, this is a plant of many uses. Its usefulness dates back to the ancient Egyptians, and its name *chicory* is derived from a similar name in Egypt. The Roman writer and naturalist Pliny (A.D. 23–79) mentions that the Egyptians consumed vast quantities of chicory. Virgil, on the other hand, noted it as a weed when he wrote, "And spreading succory chokes the rising field." Such was its importance that chicory was also mentioned by Horace and Ovid. The species name *intybus* is also derived from the Eastern name *Hendibel*. This is also the origin of the name *endive,* which is a cultivated form of a species of chicory.

The common chicory also has edible leaves that are still used in salads today. They are cut from young plants and often blanched to remove a rather bitter taste. One variety, which was developed in Belgium and is particularly tasty, is called *witlof.* Witlof chicory, also known as Belgian endive, has become such an important gourmet food in the United States that in 1983 over three thousand tons were imported. Experimental cultivation is now underway in Connecticut.

The dried root of chicory has long been known as a substitute for coffee. During World War II it was much used both as a drink on its own and as an additive to coffee. Both chicory and dandelion roots are used in this way in Europe, especially France.

Chicory is easily recognized by its blue, daisylike flowers, which open early and close again by noon, and by its sparse, erect stems with widely spaced spreading branches. The great scientist Linnaeus told the time by a "floral clock" based on the habits of the plants around him in Uppsala, Sweden. In that northern city, chicory opened at 5 A.M. and closed at 10 A.M., thus providing two of the hours on his clock for part of the year.

145

Great Burdock

Arctium lappa L.

Family: *Asteraceae*
Aster family

Additional names:
bardona, bat-weed, beggar's buttons, burdane, burr, cockle buttons, fox's clote, hardock, love leaves, stick buttons, thorn burr, vardana

People who walk in meadows and woodlands in late summer know the burdock because of the hooked burrs that cling tenaciously to their clothes, and many a dog owner has spent hours removing a tangle of burr and fur from his or her pet. That Shakespeare was well acquainted with its tenacity can be seen from these references.

> *They are burrs, I can tell you, they'll stick*
> *where they are thrown.*
> Troilus and Cressida, *III.ii.93*

> *Crown'd with rank fumiter and furrow-weeds,*
> *With burdocks, hemlock, nettles, cuckoo-flowers,*
> *Darnel, and all the idle weeds that grow*
> *In our sustaining corn.*
> King Lear, *IV.iv.3*

> *They are but burrs, cousin, thrown upon*
> *Thee in holiday foolery. If we walk not in the trodden paths,*
> *Our very petticoats will catch them.*
> As You Like It, *I.iii.11*

It is a native plant of England and continental Europe that was introduced to America by early colonists.

This plant belongs to the thistle section of the aster family. The flower leaves, or bracts, that form the green covering, or involucre, around the base of the flower of many members of the aster family become hooped and woody after the plant flowers. These form the hooks that give the burr its ability to cling to any passing animal. This is an adaptation of the plant to ensure that its seeds are effectively dispersed. The name *Arctium* is derived from the Greek *arktos* (bear) and alludes to the roughness of the burrs.

The burdock is a biennial plant. It forms leaves in the first year and does not flower until its second year.

The medicinal properties and uses of this plant were listed by Hippocrates, the father of medicine. He called it *bardona*. It is apparently mentioned in a Chinese medical treatise dating back to about 2690 B.C., the time of the reign of the Yellow Emperor. In traditional European medicine, burdock root was regarded as an excellent blood purifier and efficacious in the treatment of eczema and other skin diseases. The seeds and leaves have also been used in folk medicine. Almost all the medieval herbals tout the properties of this roadside weed.

147

Tansy

Tanacetum
vulgare
L.

Family: *Asteraceae*
Aster family

Additional name:
buttons

This European species was an early introduction to the gardens of the colonists and has escaped to become a common weed of roadsides and edges of fields. It was brought from Europe because of its many traditional and medicinal uses. It is a highly aromatic plant, two to three feet tall, with tightly compact, yellow flower heads that resemble a mass of buttons.

The name tansy is derived from the Greek *athanaton,* meaning immortal, because it was used for preserving dead bodies. It was reputedly given to Ganymede, the cupbearer of Olympus, to make him immortal. The tansy plant is a most effective insect repellent, and meat treated with tansy will not be touched by flies. Tansy was strewn on floors in medieval times, probably because of its insect-repelling properties.

At that time, it was a tradition to make tansy cakes after Lent on Easter Sunday. This was done in remembrance of the bitter herbs eaten by the Jewish people at Passover. Tansy was said to be a wholesome plant to eat after the sparse diet of fish during Lent.

The bitter taste is derived from tanacetin and a volatile oil that contains thujone. The oil is toxic to humans, but since it is volatile, it is probably not harmful to eat the fresh young leaves that are used to make tansy cakes and tansy bread and to flavor many other recipes.

The main medicinal use of tansy was as an anthelmintic for the treatment of worms. It was also used as a stimulant, an emmenagogue, and an abortifacient.

In the Middle Ages tansy was also a popular dye plant. The shoots and flowers were the source of an olive green color.

Queen Anne's Lace

Daucus carota
L.

Family: *Apiaceae*
Carrot family

Additional names:
bee's nest, wild carrot

It is hard to believe that the abundant wildflower we call Queen Anne's lace is the same botanical species as the carrot. Plant breeders took a wild species with a stringy, white taproot and crossbred it to produce the large, fleshy orange root that is now a most important vegetable.

This plant is named after Queen Anne of Denmark, the queen of James I of England. It is recorded that the queen often sat in the garden of Somerset House, which had an herb garden planted by the great herbalist John Gerard. She admired the border of wild carrots, one of Gerard's important medicinal plants, and challenged the ladies of the court to produce a lace with a pattern as beautiful as the flower of the wild carrot. The queen was the best lace maker and won the contest. This charming incident is commemorated by the popular name of the plant.

The wild carrot is a native plant of southern Europe and the Arab countries. The Greeks and Romans valued it as a medicinal plant, which led to its being introduced throughout Europe. It was brought to America by the first settlers, also on account of its medicinal properties. It is now one of the commonest plants of roadsides, waste places, and seasides, as well as being a pernicious weed of pastures. It is another attractive and useful wildflower that has also become a highly successful weed.

The colonists ate wild carrot roots, but they are only edible in their first year as they become too tough and stringy. The leaves are tasty and add to the flavor of soups and stews, and the seeds can be baked into cakes. They contain more vitamin A and E than the cultivated carrot. The carrot is rich in carotene (provitamin A), which we now know is an essential substance for good vision. So there is a factual basis for the sixteenth-century folk medicine practice of using carrot roots for the treatment of night blindness.

Canada Thistle

Cirsium arvense (L.) Scop.

Family: *Asteraceae*
Aster family

Additional names:
common thistle, field thistle

It is hard to know why the North American name blames Canada for this farmland weed. The so-called Canada thistle was introduced from Europe with grain seed and has now become a weed throughout the northern United States and Canadian provinces. It is a native plant of Europe and Asia that has been widely distributed by agriculture.

This plant's success in spreading is due to its two methods of reproducing itself. It has wind-borne, parachute-type seeds and a creeping rootstalk, so it can use either method, or both, to ensure new plants. Bits of root left in the soil after plowing or harrowing will quickly produce new plants. A single plant soon multiplies into a large patch because of the creeping rhizomes.

The long, narrow leaves of this plant are toothed and indented along their margins. Each tooth ends in a short sharp spine, which makes the plant unappealing to domestic animals. The fact that grazing animals avoid the thistles results in the weed being free to increase unimpeded.

Consequently, farmers battle to eradicate the thistle. Recently a certain level of biological control has been achieved by infecting thistle populations with a fungus called *Sclerotinia sclerotiorum*. Trials recently conducted in Montana have shown that thistle populations can be reduced by ninety-five percent by using the fungus as a control.

Aesthetically, however, the thistle is an attractive plant. The shape and texture of the prickly leaves contrast with the soft, brushlike flower. The color of the flowers varies from purple through various shades of lavender and rose to almost white.

151

Elecampane

Inula helenium L.

Family: *Asteraceae*
Aster family

Additional names:
elf dock, horseheal, scabwort, velvet dock, wild sunflower

Elecampane is an attractive sunflowerlike wildflower that makes a good garden plant, too. The leaves have a velvety pubescence on the underside. The flowers, too, are attractive, with straggly ray florets and a darker yellow mass of disc flowers. Its seeds are also liked by goldfinches and can be a means of attracting them to the garden.

It has a long history of references and uses. Elecampane is mentioned several times by both Greek and Roman writers under the name of *inula* or *enula*. Linnaeus just took the classical Latin name and turned it into the generic name for the elecampane. The Latin *inula* is thought to be a corruption of the Greek word for this plant, *helenion*. The herbalist Gerard wrote that "it took the name *helenium* from Helena, wife of Menelaus, who had her hands full of it when Paris stole her away into Phrygia." In later Latin writing it was called *Inula campana*, from which the common English name elecampane is derived.

Elecampane was often mentioned because it was regarded as an important medicinal plant. It was used as a diuretic, expectorant, antiseptic, and astringent, and for treatment of diseases of the lungs. It has been shown to contain a bactericide, helenin, that destroys the tuberculosis bacterium. It was in 1804 that the starchlike substance inulin was discovered in elecampane by the German scientist, Valentin Rose. Inulin is similar to starch, but it turns yellow instead of blue in the presence of iodine. It occurs in place of starch in many plants of the Asteraceae family. Pliny prescribed elecampane to cause mirth!

Because of its many uses, elecampane was brought to North America by early colonists. It has naturalized from Ontario and Nova Scotia south to North Carolina and west to Missouri and Minnesota. It is a common plant of fields and roadsides.

Butterfly Weed

Asclepias
tuberosa
L.

Family: *Asclepiadaceae*
Milkweed family

Additional names:
butterfly root, Canada root, Indian posy, orange swallowwort, pleurisy root

This species of the milkweed genus is a thick-stemmed plant with a tuberous root. The stem is covered with stiff, coarse hairs. This species does not have the milky juice typical of many other milkweeds. The small bright yellow-to-orange-red flowers are clustered at the top of a leaf stem. The brilliant color of the flowers attracts butterflies, which are the pollinators. After flowering spindle-shaped fruit pods are produced on an erect stem.

This plant is common from Quebec and Ontario to Florida and west to Texas and Mexico. It grows in open places, in fields, waste areas, and open woods on sandy soils.

Most of the common names refer to the roots' thick tubers because they have been popular in Native American medicine. The most common name, *pleurisy root,* arose because the root was chewed by Indians to treat pleurisy and also as an expectorant. The butterfly weed was regarded as one of the most important medicines of the Menominee Indians, who used the grated root to treat bruises and cuts. The Cherokee used a tea brewed from the root for heart trouble, but they also used it to treat many other diseases such as diarrhea and inflammation of the lungs. This is one of the most cited plants in books about the medicines of the North American Indians.

155

Wild Bergamot

Monarda fistulosa
L.

Family: *Lamiaceae*
Mint family

Additional names:
hollow-stalked monarda,
horsemint, oswego tea

This species is a member of the mint family and like most other members—such as thyme, lavender, mint, and rosemary—it is an aromatic plant that has often been used to make mint tea and as a medicinal. Another characteristic of the mint family is the square stem.

The Latin name of the plant was given by Linnaeus. He named this American genus of mints after the Spanish physician Monarda. As the squared stem is hollow, he gave it the specific name *fistulosa*.

The wild bergamot occurs from Quebec and Ontario south to Georgia and Alabama and west to Texas and Kansas. It is a plant of thickets, dry fields, and woodland borders.

The dense, round cluster of lavender-colored flowers and the pleasant scent of the plant make it an attractive garden plant that has often been cultivated. The Ojibwe Indians used the roots to make a tea for treatment of stomach ailments, and the Menominee used the leaves and inflorescence to treat catarrh.

The wild bergamot is closely related to the purple bergamot *(Monardia media)*. They can be differentiated by wild bergamot's softer, more spreading hairs on the stems and leaves and the paler flower color. This plant should not be confused with the flavor bergamot, which comes from a species of citrus, the bergamot orange.

157

Pinesap

**Monotropa
bypopitys
L.**

Family: *Monotropaceae
Indian pipe family*

Additional names:
*false beech-drops, yellow
bird's-nest*

This member of the Indian pipe family is a parasite that obtains all its nourishment, with the help of a fungus, from the roots of oaks and pines. It contains no chlorophyll, and as a result the whole plant is reddish pink, lavender, or yellow. The stem bears many thin, papery bracts instead of leaves, and the flowers at the tip are nodding and vase-shaped. They, too, are light red tinted with yellow.

The pinesap is widespread in Canada and North America and also occurs in Europe and Asia. The unusual species name simply means "beneath pines." The Greek word for a pine is *pitys,* and the pinesap is most frequently found in pine forests under the pine trees from which it can obtain its nourishment. In Europe, the pinesap is usually called *bird's nest* because of the mass of multibranched roots that is covered by the mycorrhizal fungus, which resembles a bird's nest made of twigs.

Indian Pipe

**Monotropa
uniflora
L.**

Family: *Monotropaceae
Indian pipe family*

Additional names:
*birds nest, convulsion
root, corpse plant, death
plant, fairy smoke, ice
plant*

The Indian pipe might be called a bashful parasite. Most parasites depend directly on a host for their sustenance, but the Indian pipe has found a way to obscure its dependency, so many people think it is a saprophyte and not a parasite. To obtain energy in a competitive world is always the plant's challenge. The strategy evolved by the Indian pipe is unusual and marks a regression in evolution.

Indian pipe grows on the forest floor. Many of the nearby trees have mycorrhizae (fungi) attached to their roots. These fungi speed the decay of detritus and recycle nutrients for each tree's roots to absorb. At the same time the tree helps nourish the fungi in a mutually beneficial, symbiotic relationship. This is where the parasite intrudes. Indian pipe has a small, compact root system that is entirely coated with the mycorrhizae, which in turn are attached to the tree. All the nutrition the parasite needs is tapped from the tree via the mycorrhizae.

This survival strategy has influenced the color form of the plant. It has no chlorophyll, and so it is white not green. Leaves, which the green plants need so they'll have sufficient surface area to capture light, are unnecessary; so the Indian pipe has no leaves but only scaly bracts on its stems.

The Indian pipe has been used as a medicinal plant by the American Indians. It was used as an ophthalmic for eye disorders and as a nervine for epilepsy and convulsions. The dried roots were pulverized and mixed with water to make the medicine.

This plant has a distribution ranging from Newfoundland to Washington State and south to Florida and California. This widespread distribution shows that its survival strategy has not inhibited the successful dispersal of Indian pipe through the forests of North America.

Great Blue Lobelia

Lobelia
siphilitica
L.

Family: *Lobeliaceae*
Lobelia family

Additional names:
blue cardinal flower,
high belia

This showy, blue-flowered lobelia is a close relative of the red cardinal flower. The attractive, blue flowers are borne on the stem between leaf bracts or flower leaves. The flowers have two lips, and the lower lip is striped white to form a nectar guide to attract the bee pollinators. Occasionally, pure white or blue flowers occur. It is a common species of wet meadows, swamps, and woodlands from Maine to North Carolina and west to Colorado and Texas.

As the species name indicates, this plant has been used as a remedy for syphilis. For this treatment it was used in conjunction with the roots of mayapple and the bark of wild cherry. It was the most frequently used cure for that disease in many North American Indian tribes.

The whole plant contains a poisonous, milky juice with alkaloids that cause vomiting. The Meskwaki Indians used the flowers as an inhalant for catarrh and as a love potion. They put the chopped roots into the food of an argumentative couple without their knowledge to prevent divorce and to make them love each other again! The blue lobelia and the cardinal flower are both used in homeopathic medicine.

Cardinal Flower

Lobelia
cardinalis
L.

Family: *Lobeliaceae*
Lobelia family

These tall, brilliantly red flowers linger from July until October, gracing the autumn landscape. Their color lights the wet marshy places over a wide area from Quebec and southern Ontario to Florida and the Gulf states. Although it is tempting to pick these lovely flowers, it is better to leave them rather than to reduce the wild population by picking.

Bright red, tubular flowers are usually visited by hummingbirds, and the cardinal flower is no exception. The beak of the hummingbird fits nicely into the petal tube so that the bird can drink the nectar. The stamens discharge the pollen on the inside of the tube so the probing hummingbird is dusted with it, and the flowers are pollinated as the hummingbirds dart from flower to flower. Since the pollen is released before the pistil grows up and becomes receptive to pollen, cross-pollination rather than self-fertilization takes place. The stigmatic surface is on the inside of two lobes formed by the split end of the pistil. As the pistil pushes up through the stamen tube past the anther, the stigmatic surfaces are enclosed face to face so that self-pollination cannot take place. Once past the stamens the lobes open to expose the stigmatic surface to receive pollen from the hummingbird.

Like its relative the blue lobelia, the cardinal flower was an important medicinal herb for the Native American. It was also used for the treatment of syphilis by the Cherokee and many other groups. The plant contains more of the poisonous alkaloid lobeline than the great blue lobelia. The cardinal flower was used as an anthelmintic and as an antispasmodic.

AUTUMN

Sometime at the end of August the air suddenly changes and I know that the summer is over.

The grass is yellow and tired from the summer heat. Our meadow loses its carpety quality and becomes a bushy tangle of meadowsweet, steeplebush, joe-pye weed, tansy, and goldenrod. Canadian geese are moving south. Robins are leaving, too. We decide finally to mow our meadow.

Every day I notice some changes in our beautiful scenery. Green colors disappear rapidly from the maple woods and soon we are surrounded by the bright colors of yellow, red, and orange. The whole countryside looks as if it is caught up in a huge, smokeless fire. Only evergreens keep their color and make interesting dark green patterns in this breathtaking mosaic. White farmhouses and the little church on the other side of our hill look small and dainty in this dramatic picture.

An occasional ground frost burns most of the summer flowers. Some of them disappear without leaving any visible remains, some leave their seedpods on dried stalks with spirals of dead leaves.

I love the peace of this season. I collect and paint those flowers that still bravely resist the cold nights: closed and fringed gentian, great lobelia, thistle, ladies' tresses. Various species of goldenrod and aster dominate the flora of the fall with their gold and purple tones. Colorful monarch butterflies rest and feed on goldenrods and thistles during their brave journey to warm Mexico.

162

The days of the Indian summer are still warm enough for me to swim in our nearby lake. The water feels so quiet and so clear. On the banks I can still find a few purple loosestrife plants.

The edges of the woods are full of delicious mushrooms, which I dry and pickle. We are like chipmunks, gathering herbs, fruits, and vegetables for the long, cold winter.

One day in October a strong wind comes and blows all the beauty away. The silvery stems of the maple trees look so sad and naked without their colorful coats. Only a few small trees that managed to hide in the shelter of the bigger ones still radiate their fiery colors—at least for a few days longer.

Frost is killing more plants every day. I can still find a few modest weeds that I hardly noticed before beside the more glamorous flowers: shepherd's purse, pineapple weed, chickweed. . . . In nature's ever-changing world, they give a feeling of endurance and resistance.

The ground is covered with dead leaves now. The melancholy of dying is settling into my soul. We are greeting the last flocks of geese flying over our house. It is hard to say good-bye.

But when I uncover the leaves, I can find roots and seeds in the ground. Some of them are sprouting already. They will rest for now and start to grow when their time comes. No end, only change.

Anna Vojtech

New England Aster

**Aster novae-
angliae
L.**

Family: *Asteraceae
Aster family*

Linnaeus named this aster for New England when he first described it from specimens collected in that region. It is a plant of roadsides, fields, and open woodland. Its range extends far beyond New England since it occurs from Quebec to Alaska and south to Wyoming, Arkansas, and Alabama.

Like the heart-leaved aster, it is a blue-flowered fall plant, but it is even more showy than its relative for it bears up to fifty purple-to-violet-blue or, rarely, white flowers. It grows up to eight feet tall. The stem and the leaf veins are sticky in this species, and the flower stalks are covered with glands. Because of its attractive flowers, this species has also become a garden plant, and many cultivated varieties exist in a range of blue, red, and white colors and with larger ray flowers. Bees, both in the garden and in the wild stands, are attracted to it for its food pollen.

The Ojibwe Indians use this species to attract game by smoking the leaves in a pipe to create an odor that attracts deer. The leaves were also used by various Indian tribes for the treatment of skin irritations and to alleviate the effects of poison ivy.

Grass-of-Parnassus

Parnassia glauca Raf.

Family: *Saxifragaceae Saxifrage family*

This plant belongs to a genus that was named after the Greek Mount Parnassus, where it is said the scientist Dioscorides observed the species in the wet mountain meadows. This is one of thirteen species that occur in North America; the others occur in Europe and temperate Asia and well into the Arctic zone.

The glaucous grass-of-Parnassus is a plant of calcareous bogs, shores, and damp meadows. The leaves are borne in a basal rosette, and the single white flower striped with green veins is borne on an erect, central flower stalk, or scape. There is a single, rounded, cauline leaf that clasps the flower stem and is inserted at a fifth to halfway up the length of the stem.

This species occurs from Quebec and New Brunswick south to New Jersey and Virginia and west to Iowa and South Dakota. It also is found on the West Coast in Washington State.

The flowers of the genus *Parnassia* have five fertile, pollen-bearing stamens and five sterile stamens, or staminodia, opposite the petals. Each staminodium is made up of three fused stamens, the anthers of which have become reduced to glands.

I have become well acquainted with one flower after another, and my own roots are slowly growing into the earth, which has shown me its beautiful treasure . . . the wildflowers.

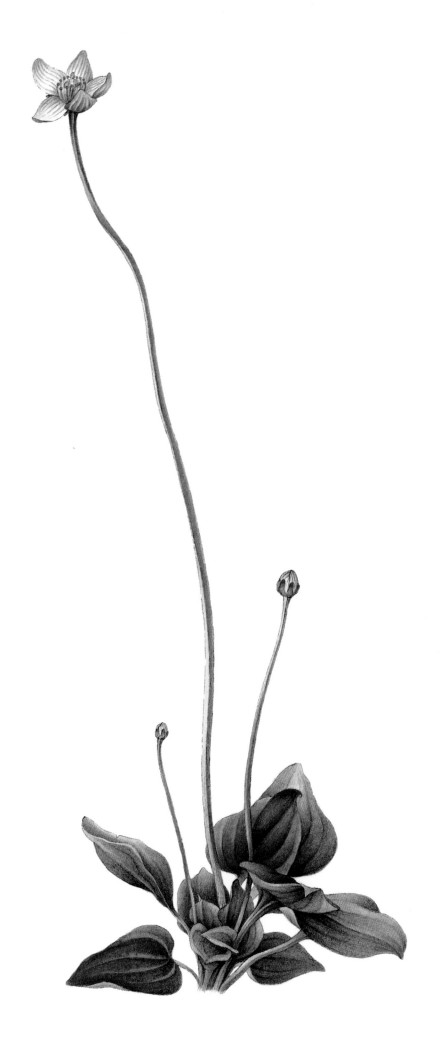

Lance-leaved Goldenrod

Solidago graminifolia (L.) Salisb.

Family: *Asteraceae*
Aster family

Additional names:
bushy goldenrod, flat-topped goldenrod, grass-leaved goldenrod

The goldenrods belong to the prolific, mainly American genus *Solidago,* which has more than one hundred species. In this book we feature three species, two in flower and a third as a dried plant. The goldenrods are associated with fall. Their show of gold, which decorates so many meadows, continues from early August until well after the first frosts, and some even linger into late November. Even in New York City eighteen species of goldenrod can be found, evidence that they are well adapted to waste places as well as roadsides, fields, and thickets. The goldenrods are often accused of the evils of another group of plants in the aster family, the ragweeds. Because the goldenrods, with their conspicuous show of yellow flowers, bloom at the same time as the much less obvious ragweeds, they are frequently blamed for the hay fever caused by the ragweeds.

The goldenrods are pollinated by insects such as the monarch butterfly and have the heavy, sticky pollen characteristic of insect-pollinated plants. The inconspicuous ragweeds, on the other hand, produce larger amounts of wind-borne pollen, the major source of summer and fall allergies.

As its name implies, the lance-leaved goldenrod has thin, narrow grasslike leaves, but it is one of several narrow-leaved species. However, the narrow leaves combined with the flat-topped flower clusters help to distinguish this species, which occurs across southern Canada and the northern United States. The different types of flower clusters are most helpful in distinguishing the different species of goldenrod. For example, compare this painting with that of the Canada goldenrod, which has flowers arranged in a pyramidal cluster.

In wildflower gardens, the lance-leaved goldenrod is an excellent plant for damp, open places on poor soil. It can even outcompete the purple loosestrife.

Canada Goldenrod

Solidago canadensis L.

Family: *Asteraceae*
Aster family

The goldenrod genus name, *Solidago,* means to make whole and was given to this genus because one species was used as an herb to heal wounds at the time of the Crusades. Many of the species of goldenrod were used as medicinal plants for a variety of ailments, especially for kidney diseases.

The Canada goldenrod is the most common of all the goldenrods. It grows from Labrador to Florida and the West Coast. It has an attractive and large plume flower cluster, which flowers from July to October and grows well in the garden, in full sun, and on well-drained soil.

Many of the plants illustrated in this book were introduced from Europe, but the goldenrod is an example of the reverse. It was taken to Europe as a garden flower and has escaped into the wild in Britain and continental Europe. It is still a popular garden flower in Europe, and horticulturists have produced many hybrids and new garden varieties of goldenrod. Some of the hybrids produced in England have later been returned to the gardens of North America. The goldenrod is such a characteristic and popular American flower that many times when a national flower has been discussed in Congress, it has been proposed as a strong candidate.

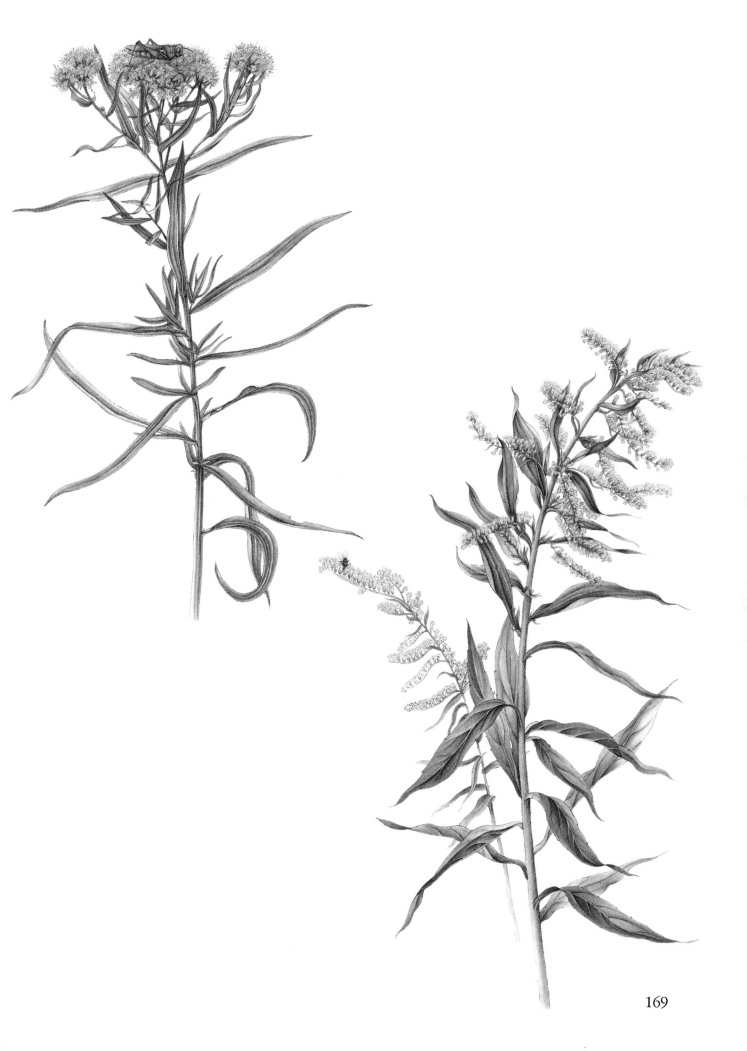

169

Heart-leaved Aster

Aster cordifolius L.

Family: *Asteraceae Aster family*

Additional names: *bee weed, branching aster, common blue wood aster, tongue*

This bushy plant grows in woods and thickets and can attain heights of up to six feet. It has leaves with heart-shaped bases that are coarse and rough like a tongue in texture. The upper leaves clasp the stem, and the larger, lower leaves have short and hairy stems. In late September a mass of blue flowers is produced. The outer ray flowers have fourteen to twenty lavender-to-pale-blue or whitish petals.

The heart-leaved aster has a range from Nova Scotia south to Georgia and west to Minnesota. It is a common woodland flower. The whole plant is quite aromatic and has been used as an aromatic nervine. The leaves are crushed, and the aromatic smell is used to calm spasms and hysteria. The Flambeau Ojibwe use this species as a hunting charm to attract deer. It is one of several plants whose leaves are smoked in a pipe to attract deer for hunting.

Tall White Lettuce

Prenanthes altissima L.

Family: *Asteraceae Aster family*

Additional name: *rattlesnake root*

Many of the late-summer and fall plants pictured here belong to the aster family. This large family is the most important of all the fall-flowering plant groups. The tall white lettuce is one of several species in this genus. It grows in damp, shady places and along the edges of dark woods and thickets from Maine to Georgia. It is a coarse plant with a milky juice. The leaves are triangular and have earlike lobes at their bases. The leaves at different positions on the stem are quite different in shape; the lower ones are wedge shaped and the upper leaves vary from a heart shape to a long, pointed oval shape.

The flowering heads are white and contain five to eighteen flowers each. They hang on short stalks and droop down close to the purplish stem in small irregular groups. The blossoms are small and look out of proportion to the robust stalk. All species of white lettuce, or rattlesnake root, have only the one type of drooping flower head.

This species has been used as a cure for snakebites and as a contraceptive. The Iroquois thought that the tall white lettuce was the female plant, and that another species, white rattlesnake root *(P. alba)*, was the male of the same plant. They mixed these together as a medicine.

The true lettuce belongs to a closely related genus, *Lactuca*. The wild species of *Lactuca* also have a milky sap like *Prenanthes*. The process of cultivation has gradually removed the white sap and the bitter taste to make it more palatable. The tall white lettuce is too bitter to be considered edible except as a medicine.

171

Fringed Gentian

**Gentiana crinita
Froel.**

Family: *Gentianaceae
Gentian family*

There are many species of gentian in North America. The eastern fringed gentian occurs from Quebec to Minnesota and south to Georgia and Iowa. The combination of vivid blue color and delicate fringes on the petals makes this a most appealing flower. It is also welcome because it is a late bloomer that waits until October to burst into flower. In fact, it has proved too appealing and has become rare through excess picking of the flowers and collection of the seeds for growing. Since it is a biennial plant, the picking of the flowers prevents the formation of seeds to form the next generation. This is a plant to enjoy in the field rather than collect, and it should be grown in the garden only from seeds from a cultivated source.

The fringed gentian is a plant of wet places in seepage areas and meadows. But it is a mysterious plant because one year it may occur in abundance in a particular meadow, and the next year it does not appear at all. The dustlike seed may have been blown far from the parent plants. This erratic habit makes the gentian an even more appealing plant.

The genus was named for King Gentius of Illyria. It is said that this king of the Balkan peninsula discovered the medicinal properties of a species of gentian.

This species is one of several gentians with fringed petals; for example, *G. barbellata,* which is from the Rockies and has silvery leaves, and the small fringed gentian, *G. procera,* of the midwest.

Peppermint

**Mentha piperita
L.**

Family: *Lamiaceae
Mint family*

Additional name:
brandy mint

We have found many ways to use this plant, with its pleasant, cool flavor. We put it in drinks to make mint juleps, cook it to make mint jelly to eat with lamb, and use it to flavor cigarettes. It is menthol that gives peppermint its flavor. Menthol acts physiologically to dilate the blood vessels and consequently creates a sensation of coolness as well as giving a distinctive flavor.

The peppermint is a European hybrid cultigen produced from a cross between spearmint *(Mentha spicata)* and water mint *(Mentha aquatica).* Because of its great importance as a medicine and flavor, it was brought over by the early colonists and has escaped so that it now occurs all over North America. The ancient Greeks and Romans used spearmint, and the hybrid peppermint was first recognized as a separate entity by the famous English botanist John Ray in 1696. It quickly became an important medicinal plant. However, it had been used much earlier and was certainly not a recent hybrid when Ray first described it.

Peppermint is cultivated in many European countries as well as in the United States, especially Michigan, Indiana, and western New York. The whole shoot of the plant is cut and harvested in July, just before flowering, and it is then steam-distilled to extract the oil of peppermint that is used so widely in the food and beverage industry. As with many other essential oils, the quality of the oil depends on the conditions under which the plant was grown.

There is a Greek legend about mint. It tells of the underworld god Pluto, who fell in love with the nymph Menthe. This so angered his wife Persephone that she turned the nymph into an herb and banished her to the swamps. The genus name *Mentha* commemorates the legend and suggests a mythical reason for the habitat of the peppermint: marshes, ditches, streamsides, and damp meadows.

Live-Forever

**Sedum telephium
L.**

Family: *Crassulaceae
Sedum family*

Additional names:
*Aaron's rod, live long,
midsummer men, orpine*

Stonecrops, the British family name for *Sedum,* have long been favorites of gardeners in Europe and America. They have introduced many species of the genus *Sedum* from one region to another, including this species, popularly known as *live-forever* or *orpine.* Although at least six species of stonecrop are native to the eastern states, several others from Europe are naturalized. Live-forever is now one of the most common species and is even a weed in some areas because it is very persistent. A small piece of stem or a leaf can form a new plant. This tenacity for life has given the common name to this plant.

In England this is called *midsummer men* because the country girls used to set up two stems, one for themselves and the other for their lover. The faithfulness of the lover was determined by the way in which his plant turned toward hers.

A decoction of the mucilaginous leaves of live-forever has been used as a popular remedy for diarrhea.

Steeplebush

**Spiraea
tomentosa
L.**

Family: *Rosaceae
Rose family*

Additional names:
*hardhack, poor man's
soap, silver leaf, spice
hardhack, white cap,
white leaf*

The flowers of this species are borne in a narrow, conical inflorescence at the top of the stem. They resemble miniature steeples colored bright pink or sometimes white. This shrub, about three feet in height, occurs from Nova Scotia south to Georgia and west to Minnesota and Arkansas. It is a common inhabitant of swamps, wet meadows, and old fields. The stems are woolly, and the leaf undersides are covered with a dense, white, woolly pubescence that gives it common names such as *silver leaf.* The flowers on the steeplebush bloom from the top downward over a considerable period of time, from July through September, so that the entire inflorescence is never in flower at the same time. The gradual flowering means that the steeplebush is less popular with gardeners than are the other popularity cultivated members of the *Spiraea* genus.

The steeplebush is rich in tannins and as a consequence was used by many native peoples. The Mohegan used a tea from the leaves as a cure for dysentery, and the Ojibwe used it for sickness during pregnancy.

Shepherd's Purse

Capsella bursa-pastoris (L.) Medic.

Family: *Brassicaceae*
Mustard family

Additional names:
mother's heart, pepper-and-salt, pepper grass, shepherd's bag, witches pouches

This plant received its popular and common names from its heart-shaped seedpods, which resemble the small leather purses used by the shepherds of medieval Europe. This European weed has been carried around the world wherever colonists have traveled, and it is ubiquitous in North America.

The leaves have a peppery flavor that is characteristic of most members of the mustard family, and they have often been used in salad. They are rich in vitamins A and C and contain twice as much of each per unit of weight as an orange. Shepherd's purse has also long been a chosen medicinal plant in Europe, especially to stop internal and external bleeding and for the treatment of diarrhea. Although the colonists introduced this plant, it was soon adopted into the pharmacopeia of the North American Indians. The seeds were made into a tea for the treatment of worms by the Mohegans, and the leaves were used to treat poison ivy by the Menominee.

The most remarkable feature of shepherd's purse is its tiny seeds, which are contained in the purselike seed capsules. As the seeds germinate they emit a sticky, gelatinous substance. This traps small insect larvae, which are then digested. The nourishment provided by the captured insects compensates for the fact that the seeds are small and contain few nutrients for the seedling. The shepherd's purse is, therefore, an insectivorous plant.

Pineapple Weed

Matricaria matricarioides (Less.) Porter

Family: *Asteraceae*
Aster family

This North American relative of a well-known European medicinal plant, chamomile, is a native of the West Coast from Alaska to Baja California. It was introduced in the east, where together with its cousin chamomile, it has naturalized along roadsides, on farms, in pastures, and in waste places. It differs from chamomile in that it has no ray flowers. The flower heads are a conical mass of disc flowers that resembles a miniature pineapple. This, combined with its pineapplelike scent, led to the common name. The name of the genus is derived from the Latin *mater,* meaning mother, a term given to plants of medicinal value. Chamomile is a most important medicinal plant in Europe, and it is still used widely to make a mildly soporific tea.

The Native American uses for this plant come from the West Coast. The Aleuts used an infusion of the leaf as an analgesic, a laxative, and to ease stomach problems. Many other tribes used the pineapple weed in their medicine. The Eskimos used dried flower heads as a remedy for colds. It is interesting that many of these western American medicinal uses for pineapple weed are similar to the European uses for chamomile.

Beggar-Ticks

***Bidens frondosus
L.***

Family: *Asteraceae
Aster family*

Additional name:
frondose bur marigold

This widespread member of the bur marigold genus occurs from Newfoundland and Nova Scotia south to Virginia and Louisiana and west to California. It is an annual plant that grows usually in wet places in meadows and ditches, but it is sometimes also found in drier waste areas.

The various species of bur marigolds are widespread because the hooks on the fruit make them catch on the fur of animals so they are easily carried around. The pappus consists of two reflexed or barbed bristles that cause the seed to cling to animals. The common name *beggar-ticks* shows how effective the plant is in getting its seeds moved around by covering the clothing of any person passing through a clump of these plants on a fall walk.

The Lumbee Indians made a decoction of the shoots of beggar-ticks and used it for the treatment of backache and headache.

WINTER

I said good-bye to the flowers, but I can't say good-bye to painting them. And this urge inspires me to continue to paint flowers even in winter when snow covers the ground.

A whole new world of incredible wealth, of the most fantastic shapes and forms and also colors, opens for me in those dried remains of wildflowers.

Some of them are difficult to identify because their seedpods are so different from their blossoms. The delicate lily of the valley, like flowers of spreading dogbane, change into long, aggressive-looking seedpods. The modest, purplish blossoms of fireweed are transformed into the most intricate labyrinth of spirals. The seedpods of a Canada lily stand upward instead of hanging down like their blossoms. It requires a lot of careful observation to be able to recognize most of my flower friends.

A fire in the wood stove, the beautiful music from my records, my lovely children playing in the living room, and snow slowly falling outside give me a feeling of peace. I don't need the refrigerator for my models; they won't wilt in front of my eyes anymore. I can take my time to paint them without feeling the pressure of time and season.

I paint on handmade paper stretched on a wooden board. I make a quick rough sketch with a pencil. Then I very carefully study and draw the flower with pen and ink. I use an old-fashioned penholder and nib with china ink. The very detailed black-and-white drawings I then color with watercolors. My brushes aren't as small as you might think, but they have to have a very good point. Very small brushes don't hold enough color.

I can work on paintings of live flowers only during daylight. Most of the flowers close their blossoms at night, and artificial light changes their color. But dried plants I can paint late in the evening. What a luxury not to be constantly interrupted!

Dried flowers give me a sense of peace, but they lack the energy of pulsing life. After the long winter I look forward to the coming of spring and the awakening of new life again.

Anna Vojtech

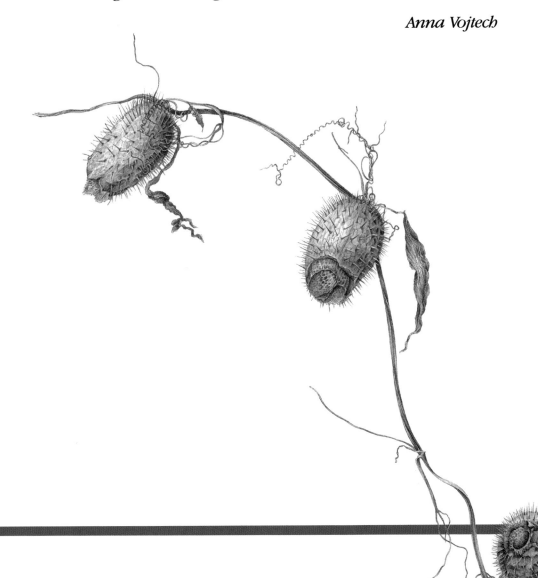

Cotton Milkweed

Asclepias syriaca L.

Family: *Asclepiadaceae Milkweed family*

Additional names: *silky sallowwort, Virginia silk, wild asparagus, wild cotton*

The delicate curves of the milkweed pods in the fields echo the lines made by the wings of the migrating birds of autumn in the skies. In the fall, the pods change gradually from green to brown, and when they are ripe they split open along one side. The numerous seeds are overlapped like the scales of a fish, and each has tightly packed tufted hair. As the seeds escape from the pods, each is borne into the air on its tuft of white, parachutelike hairs by the autumn winds.

The seed hairs, or floss, are soft, delicate fibers that are similar to kapok. During World War II, when there was a shortage of tropical kapok, which was produced mainly in Java, the milkweed floss became important and was used as a substitute to stuff life vests, the "Mae Wests" that saved many people from drowning. At that time, much of the floss was collected by Canadian schoolchildren as their contribution to the war. Apart from its use at that time, milkweed floss has not become an important product.

The milkweed plant contains another source of fiber in the stem that can be used to make paper. Although used experimentally, it is not an economic proposition at present. Another potential use for milkweed lies in the extraction of oil and polyphenol from the seeds. They contain six percent oil and seven percent polyphenol, both of which can be used for fuel. This has been researched, but milkweed has not been used commercially yet. There is potential, however, for economic uses of this common weedy species, and in the future it could become an important crop plant.

The common milkweed grows abundantly in fields and meadows and along roadsides from New Brunswick to Georgia.

Indian Pipe

**Monotropa
uniflora
L.**

Family: *Monotropaceae
Indian pipe family*

Additional names:
*bird's nest, convulsion
root, corpse plant, death
plant, fairy smoke, ice
plant*

The Indian pipe produces a single nodding flower at the end of its white stem. The other common species of *Monotropa,* the pinesap *(M. hypopitys),* has several vaselike flowers. The Indian pipe is related to the heaths and heathers and has often been placed in the family Ericaceae. Although its parasitic growth form makes it appear different, the flower structure betrays its relationship with the heath family. It has the bell-shaped flowers characteristic of most members of the family Ericaceae.

After flowering is over, the ovoid fruit capsule of the Indian pipe becomes enlarged and erect, and the plant gradually turns dark brown. The remnants of the stalk and capsule decorate the woodlands well into the winter.

Pink Lady's Slipper

**Cypripedium
acaule
Ait.**

Family: *Orchidaceae
Orchid family*

Additional names:
*Indian moccasin,
moccasin flower, nerve
root, old-goose, squirrel's
shoes, stemless lady's
slipper*

Who would have thought that the beautiful pink lady's slipper orchid would also add to the winter beauty of the forest floor. After the flowering is over, a seed capsule is formed that contains thousands of dustlike seeds that resemble pollen more than seeds because of their small size. The seed capsule remains on its single long stem. It is often hard to see, well disguised among the brown leaves of fall.

Wild Yellow Lily

Lilium canadense L.

Family: *Liliaceae*
Lily family

Additional names:
Canada lily, meadow lily

This common lily is a beautiful flower of the early summer, and its seed capsules have their own beauty in autumn. After flowering the clusters of hanging bell-shaped flowers develop into seed capsules. Although this plant produces these seed capsules to begin new plants, like many other bulbous plants it also reproduces by the production of new bulbs at the end of the underground rootstock. This enables the plant to creep gradually from one spot to another and explains why it can form large patches when it is cultivated in the garden.

Although various Indian groups ate the bulbs as food, this should not be done today as it reduces the natural populations of this attractive member of our flora.

Thimbleweed

Anemone virginiana L.

Family: *Ranunculaceae*
Buttercup family

Additional name:
tall anemone

This elegant anemone is quite distinctive because the numerous pistils in the center of the flower form a cylindrical, green, thimblelike structure. The structure persists when the plant is in the fruiting condition and can be dried and preserved.

This is a summer-flowering anemone. It has greenish white flowers. It occurs in open woods, prairies, and thickets, and grows up to three feet in height. Each stem bears from three to nine flowers. It is found from central Maine and Quebec to Georgia and west to Arkansas, Kansas, and Minnesota.

Meadowsweet

Spiraea latifolia (Ait.) Borkh.

Family: *Rosaceae*
Rose family

Meadowsweet is a low shrub that grows up to five feet tall, and in summer the branches terminate in a dense, pyramidal cluster of white-to-pale-pink flowers. The brown fruit, which follows the flowers, does not fall but splits open along one side to release the seeds; but they then remain in the old flower cluster, forming an illusion of a brown winter bloom.

This is a plant of meadows and old fields and moist or dry upland places. It grows from Newfoundland and Quebec to North Carolina and west to Missouri and South Dakota. At higher altitudes in the mountains of New England, the inflorescence is small and little branched and not of the characteristic pyramidal shape.

The leaves of meadowsweet make an agreeable tea. This tea is an old herbal remedy of many Native American groups used to prevent nausea and vomiting. It is astringent because of its tannin content.

Pearly Everlasting

Anaphalis margaritacea (L.) Benth. and Hook. ex Clarke

Family: *Asteraceae*
Aster family

Additional names:

cotton weed, Indian posy, Indian tobacco, life everlasting, moonshine, none-so-pretty, poverty weed, silver button, silver leaf

The name *pearly everlasting* suggests why this flower features as one of the dried plants. The pearly everlasting is quite unusual among our wildflowers because if it is picked while the flowers are young, it will dry and look the same as the fresh plant for at least a year. The small, tightly clustered flower heads are pearly white with yellow centers. The white part consists of numerous papery scalelike bracts that will last indefinitely, and the yellow flowers are in the center. A bouquet of this plant is made more attractive by the white, loose woolly covering of the stem and the white, woolly underside of the leaves.

The pearly everlasting is found from Labrador and Newfoundland to Alaska and the Aleutian Islands, and from New England to California. It is native to Asia. It grows in open, dry places, especially in burned and cutover areas and mountain habitats.

The numerous local names reflect its many uses. The Indians and New England fishermen used the leaves as a tobacco substitute. It was well known as a healing dressing for wounds because of the cottony wool on the leaves. The leaves were also used for treatment of ulcers and mouth sores. Decoctions of the pearly everlasting had many medicinal uses, mainly because of its strong astringent properties. It was also a magic plant of the Menominee, who used it in a smudge to discourage the haunting return of the ghost of a deceased member of their tribe. A smudge together with a beaver's gallbladder was used to bring a person who had fainted back to consciousness.

Because it is abundant and spreads easily, it is an excellent plant to gather and enjoy at home in the winter.

189

Common Cattail

**Typha latifolia
L.**

Family: *Typhaceae
Cattail family*

Additional names:
*black cap, bulrush,
candlewick, cat-o'-nine-
tails, flag, flagtail, marsh
beetle, reed mace, water
torch*

Large stands of cattails are a familiar sight to anyone who has traveled through the eastern states. It is a species that occurs in fresh water marshes throughout the North Temperate Zone in America, Europe, and Asia. It forms large colonies because of its capacity to spread by its creeping rootstock.

"The supermarket of the swamp" is a name it has been given. Almost all parts of the plant are edible at some stage of their development. Cattail hearts from the young, white inner stem are like asparagus. The young bloom can be eaten like corn in its early stages before the pollen develops, and the starchy roots can be used like potatoes. Even the pollen can be collected in early summer and used as flour to make bread and cakes.

The clublike head of the cattail consists of an upper spike of male flowers with a cylinder of brown female flowers directly below it. The fluff that surrounds the seeds in this part of the head has often been used as a stuffing fiber for pillows, furniture, heat insulators, life preservers, and many other padded objects. The flat, swordlike leaves were used as basket-making and rushing fiber.

The Indians had so many uses for cattails that it is hard to list them. The down was used in warfare like tear gas. The down was also mixed with egg yolks as a treatment for burns. The Apache used the pollen, which they regarded as sacred, in the puberty rites of young girls. The medicine man mixed pollen, grass, and water and sprinkled the mixture on the girl and then on the surrounding crowd. The Hopi mixed the down with tallow to make a chewing-gumlike substance. They also used the down for candlewicks and boat caulking. Because of its prolific growth, many people have proposed the use of cattails as a source of fuel, and this may well come about as fossil fuel reserves diminish.

If you want to dry cattails to enjoy them in the winter, they must be collected in early summer before the downy seeds have developed. Cut them and hang them upside down to dry until you want them for your arrangement.

This plant has many uses for humans, but apart from its usefulness it graces the landscape with its regal beauty and generously hosts large flocks of birds, offering them food and shelter.

191

Virgin's Bower

Clematis virginiana L.

Family: *Ranunculaceae Buttercup family*

Additional names:
devil's darning needle, devil's hair, love-vine, traveller's joy, wild clematis, wild hops, woodbine

This climbing vine belongs to the same genus as the popular garden clematis. It has many small white flowers that are much less conspicuous than those of its cultivated cousins. However, after flowering the fruits grow long, feathery tailed plumes. The dense clusters look like delicate frosted flowers on the autumn and winter thickets.

It grows along roadside hedges, riversides, borders of woods, and thickets from Nova Scotia south to Georgia and Louisiana.

This species, unlike other species of clematis, does not have tendrils to assist its climbing habit. Instead, the stems and the leafstalks twist and wrap around other plants. Ruskin called this a "gadding vine" because it runs riot on walls, hedges, and other vegetation.

Take care if you want to collect this plant for a dried arrangement because it causes severe dermatitis and blistering of the skin.

I have a companion in my work. His name is Frost. On very cold winter days he paints the most fantastic flowers on our windows. He is the true artist. Like all nature he does his art just for this moment, and then it disappears. I see how through my paintings I want to preserve the art of nature.

193

Curled Dock

Rumex crispus L.

Family: *Polygonaceae Buckwheat family*

Additional names: *sour dock, yellow dock*

The beauty of late-autumn fields and hedgerows is enhanced by the subtle colors and shapes of the seed heads and pods of many plants. The dense cluster of dark brown seeds of the curled dock, each with its three wings, makes its own contribution.

This species and several of the other common docks of North America were introduced from Europe as weeds of grain seed. These European weeds soon became common throughout the United States and adjacent Canada.

This species' leaves have exceptionally wavy, or crisped, margins, giving it the name *curled* or *curly dock*. The docks have been much used in local medicine, and the roots of the curled dock were commonly employed as a laxative. The leaves were used for treatment of many skin complaints and as an astringent to stop bleeding and treat hemorrhoids and cuts. In Europe the leaves are often used to alleviate the sting of nettles (genus *Urtica)*, with considerable effect. The young leaves of this and other species of dock are commonly used as spring greens. However, a word of caution is in order because this plant causes dermatitis in people who are allergic to it.

Wild Cucumber

Echinocystis lobata (Michx.) Torr. & Gray

Family: *Cucurbitaceae Cucumber family*

Additional names: *burr cucumber, wild balsam apple*

This vine in the cucumber family has a widespread distribution from New Brunswick to Florida and west to Saskatchewan and Texas. This species produces two kinds of flowers on the same plant. The male flowers are produced in large compound clusters that can be up to a foot long, whereas the female flowers are solitary or in groups of two or three. These white female flowers produce the oval and spinous fruit that gives the genus name to the plant. Its name comes from two Greek words: *echinos,* a hedgehog, and *cystos,* a bladder, both used to describe its spiny and inflated fruit. The leaves are maple-like, or lobed, which is reflected in the species name, *lobata.*

This plant is interesting because its three-forked tendrils are very sensitive and twine rapidly, but as they come around toward the main axis of the plant they become straight and erect, thus avoiding contact with it and preventing them from twining onto themselves.

The wild cucumber has often been cultivated because of its quick growth and its long flowering period, which runs from June through October.

The spiny fruit makes this an attractive dried plant. When ripe, the fruit bursts open at the top, and four large black seeds, about the size of watermelon seeds, are released. Although this vine belongs to the cucumber and melon family, its fruit is not edible.

Bull Thistle

Cirsium vulgare
(Savi) Tenore

Family: *Asteraceae*
Aster family

Additional names:
common thistle, horse thistle

Like most of the common thistles in North America, this is a European weed that was introduced with seed. It now occurs almost wherever there is agriculture. The bull thistle is larger than the Canada thistle, and it has a large taproot rather than a creeping root. This is a biennial plant that forms a rosette of leaves the first year and flowers the second. Because of its growth habit and lack of vegetative shoots from the roots, this plant is much easier to control than the Canada thistle.

The flower heads are showy and purple and attract both bees and butterflies in large numbers. They bloom over a long period, from June until early fall.

This dried flower head serves to remind us that nothing in nature is wasted. Summer's purple flowers are transformed into a mass of downy parachutes that can carry the plant's fruits, containing the seeds, to new ground. The down is a favorite nest-building material of goldfinches, which unlike most other birds wait until summer to build their nests. They also eat the seeds.

197

Spotted Joe-Pye Weed

Eupatorium maculatum L.

Family: *Asteraceae*
Aster family

Joe-pye weed is the name given to some species of the large genus *Eupatorium*. They were named after an Indian whose real name was Zhopai. He was a medicine man who befriended the early colonists of the Massachusetts Bay Colony when they fell sick with typhus. The treatment with joe-pye weed helped the patients to break out in a sweat and recover from the disease. The sad sequence to this incident was that his large tract of land was taken from him by the colonists whom he had cured. As Zhopai became a legend his name was anglicized to Joe Pye, and the plant he used in his cure was called the joe-pye weed. Joe-pye weed was used by various groups of Indians to cure many diseases, and it soon became an important medicinal plant of the settlers.

The genus *Eupatorium* was named after the King of Pontus, Mithradates Eupator (120–63 B.C.). He was a scholar and a tyrant who defended his territory against the Romans. He was a skilled medicine man who, when poisoned by his own mother, recovered by taking an antidote made from a species of the joe-pye weed genus that now bears his name. He continued to take daily doses for the rest of his life. The species name, *maculatum*, refers to the spotted stem that distinguishes this species.

The spotted joe-pye weed is one of several closely related species. It differs from the sweet joe-pye weed *(E. purpureum)* in its flat-topped cluster of pinkish flowers and in the purple or purple-spotted stem. It is a widespread plant across southern Canada and the northern states and south to North Carolina. It is found in damp meadows and thickets, and after flowering from July through September the fuzzy flower heads can be dried to become an attractive part of a winter flower arrangement.

Early Goldenrod

Solidago juncea Ait.

Family: *Asteraceae*
Aster family

Additional name:
plume goldenrod

The third species of goldenrod in this book is shown as a dried flower because most goldenrod species are beautiful in their dried state.

The early goldenrod is distributed from Newfoundland to Georgia. It is found in dry or moist, open places, by roadsides, and in thickets.

The leaves in the basal clump are large and broad, and the stem leaves become progressively smaller as they grow out of the purple stem toward the flower cluster. This species has a spreading flower cluster, and when it turns to seed or is dried it resembles a mass of feathers, hence the name *plume goldenrod*. The plant flowers from July until late fall. It is only found in its dried state in the early winter.

Spreading Dogbane

Apocynum andro-saemifolium L.

Family: *Apocynaceae Dogbane family*

Additional names: *bitter root, fly trap, honey bloom, wild ipecac*

This is a low shrub with spreading forked branches that grow out in all directions. The pink, tubular flowers are slightly nodding and after pollination produce the paired pod-like fruit characteristic of members of the dogbane family. Inside the pod are the seeds, surrounded by a parachute of downy fiber. This species occurs from Newfoundland to Georgia and across the continent to British Columbia, Alaska, and California. It is a plant of fields, roadsides, and dry thickets.

The scientific name of the genus means the same as the common English name *dogbane* and is derived from the Greek *apo,* meaning from, and *kunos,* a dog. It is said to be especially toxic to dogs. Like most members of the dogbane family, the entire plant contains milky latex that caused the Potawatomi Indians to call it "women's breast weed." The latex causes severe skin blisters in some people, while others can handle the plant with impunity.

This plant can be used in many ways. The bark of the stem provides a fine fiber that was used by many Indian tribes as their best sewing thread. It was also used to make cord, and the Menominee made their bow strings from dogbane. A related species, Indian hemp *(A. cannabinum)* was much used for cordage, fishing nets, string bags, and coarse material. The medicinal uses of this plant could fill many pages. The roots were used as an emetic similar to ipecac, and it is sometimes called *ipecac.* The plant contains glycosides, which have an effect similar to digitalis.

Small flies in search of nectar from the flowers insert their proboscises into a cavity between the stamens, but often get them stuck. As they struggle to escape they become more firmly lodged and eventually die. This is the reason that *fly trap* is another common name for dogbane.

201

Glossary

Following are definitions of some of the botanical and medical terms used in the text.

abortifacient A plant causing the abortion of a foetus.

anther The terminal, saclike part of a stamen that bears the pollen.

astringent A medicine, usually bitter tasting, that contracts soft or relaxed parts of the body. The commonest are tannins.

biennial A plant that takes two years to complete its life cycle, usually producing a rosette of leaves the first year and flowers and fruit only in the second year.

bracts Modified leaves that are situated at the base of an inflorescence. They are usually smaller than ordinary leaves and are often colored, such as those of the dogwood flower.

bulb An underground storage organ consisting of a flattened stem with basal roots and fleshy leaves surrounded by protective scale leaves. It often is the means of vegetative reproduction.

carminative A medicine that expels gas from the stomach and intestines.

cathartic A purgative used to provoke a bowel movement.

cleistogamy The production of seeds through self-pollination in a closed flower that never opens, as occurs in many violets.

composite flower A cluster of reduced flowers that forms a single flowerlike head, as can be seen in members of the aster family.

compound leaf A leaf that is divided into a number of smaller leaflets.

corona A crownlike structure of the petals of some flowers, such as those of the milkweed family.

corm A fleshy, underground stem resembling a bulb, as in a crocus.

cross-pollination The transfer of pollen from one plant to a different one of the same species causing fertilization.

diaphoretic A substance that produces or increases perspiration.

dioecy The phenomenon of bearing male and female flowers on different individual plants.

disc flower The small, tubular central flowers of a composite flower, as are found in the brown center of the black-eyed Susan.

emetic A substance that causes vomiting.

emmenagogue A medicine used to promote menstrual discharge.

filament The slender threadlike stalk of a stamen.

heterostyly The phenomenon of having stamens and styles of different lengths on different plants to encourage cross-pollination. Distylous plants have two flower types, as in bluets, and tristylous ones have three.

inflorescence The cluster of flowers on a plant.

keel The two lower petals of a flower of the pea family that are united into a boatlike structure.

latex The milky white sap of many plants, such as in the milkweeds or dandelions.

leaflet One of the leaflike parts of a compound leaf.

nectar The sugary solution secreted by the nectaries of many flowers as a food for their pollinators.

pappus A bristle or group of bristles on the seeds of members of the daisy family, which often act as a parachute for wind dispersal, as in dandelion and coltsfoot.

pectoral A medicine used for the treatment of ailments of the chest and lungs.

perianth The collective term for the petals and sepals of a flower.

petal The usually brightly colored, inner whorl or whorls of the perianth of a flower.

pistil The female part of a flower, composed of an ovary, style, and stigma.

pollen The male spores of a plant, which are produced in the anthers of the stamens.

pollination The transfer of pollen from the anther to the stigma of a flower.

protandry The process whereby the pollen is produced before the stigma is receptive to avoid self-pollination.

protogyny The process whereby the stigma is receptive before the release of pollen to avoid self-pollination.

ray flower The outer petallike flowers of a composite flower, such as the white outer ring of flowers of an oxeye daisy.

rhizome An underground stem that grows horizontally and is often enlarged as a winter food-storage organ.

sepal The usually green outer whorl of the perianth of a flower that frequently has a protective function for the bud but sometimes resembles a petal, as in iris flowers.

sessile An organ, such as a leaf, without a stalk.

spadix The flower spike of members of the Arum lily family that is enclosed in a spathe.

spathe A large flower bract or pair of bracts that encloses the inflorescence, as in the Arum lily family.

spur A narrow, tubular structure, usually a modified petal, that contains nectar at its base to feed the pollinator, as in many species of orchids and dutchman's breeches.

stamen The male part of the flower, consisting of a filament and an anther.

staminodium A modified stamen that is not fertile and does not produce viable pollen.

standard The upper, showy part of a pea flower (also called a banner) or a petal of an iris flower.

stigma The area of the pistil that receives pollen, usually sticky and located at the apex of the style.

stipules Small appendages usually at the base of the leafstalk that are leaflike or scalelike.

style The part of the pistil that connects the ovary and the stigma.

tannin A yellowish astringent substance that occurs naturally in many plants and is used for tanning leather and in medicines.

Index of Scientific Names

Index of
Common Names

General Index

cardiac glycosides, 96
carminative, 22
carnivorous plant, 118
carotene, 100, 148
carrot, 74, 148
catarrh, 12, 156, 160
cathartic, 14, 94, 112, 128
cattle fodder, 100, 104
chamomile, 102, 176
cheese, 94
Cherokee Indians, 98, 122,
    154, 160
Chile, 32, 122
Chippewa Indians, 22, 70,
    112, 132, 142
chlorophyll, 158
chromosomes, 22, 88
Clayton, John, 22
cleistogamy, 92, 130
Clinton, DeWitt, 44
composite flower, 102
compound leaf, 48, 58
conservation, 8, 9, 14
contraceptive, 42, 96, 170
convulsions, 12, 28, 158
cordage, 200
corm, 14, 42
corydine, 28
cosmic radiation, 88
coughs, 20, 96, 120, 124
Cowley, 74
Cree Indians, 52
cross-fertilization, 48, 114
cross-pollination, 26, 92, 130,
    136
cryptopine, 28
cucumber, 130, 194
Culpeper, 20, 120
Cymbeline, 108
cytoplasm, 88

Dacey, John W. H., 54
dandelion
    coffee, 36
    salad, 36
    wine, 36
Darwin, Charles, 118
daylily, 126
deer attractant, 28, 164, 170
Deptford, 110
dermatitis, 24, 26, 50, 192,
    194
dewberry, 72
diaphoretic, 22
diarrhea, 56, 72, 108, 154,
    174, 176
digitalis, 200
dioecy, 48
Dioscorides, 20, 82, 94, 166
diosgenin, 16, 44
disc flowers, 102, 142, 152, 176

dispersal, 130, 138, 180
diuretic, 22, 36, 94, 102, 112,
    130, 152
doctrine of signatures, 140
dogs, 44, 200
dumb cane, 42
dye, 24, 36, 72, 78, 94, 112,
    122, 132, 148
dysentery, 56, 174

earache, 142
eczema, 122, 146
Edward III, 78, 94
Egyptians, 144
elaiosome, 28
emergency food, 124
emetic, 14, 80, 94, 122, 200
emmenagogue, 148
endive, 144
epilepsy, 158
Eskimos, 176
everlasting, 188
expectorant, 14, 16, 38, 56,
    108, 152, 154
explosive fruit, 130, 138
extinction, 118
eye disorders, 32, 108, 158

Farrer, Reginald, 90
fat catabolism, 112
fecogenin, 16
fever, 80, 124
fiber, 182, 190, 200
fishing nets, 200
Flambeau Ojibwe, 170
fleur-de-lys, 78
floral biology, 86
floral clock, 144
Flora of Virginia, 22
fuel, 182, 190
fulling, 136
fungicidal, 130
fungus, 150, 158

Ganymede, 148
garden flower, 156, 164, 168
garden pea, 58
Gaspé Peninsula, 16
Gentius, King, 172
Gerard, John, 20, 32, 40, 148,
    152
germidine, 80
germitrine, 80
gill tea, 32
gloriosa daisy, 142
glycosides, 200
goldfinches, 20, 84, 152, 196
greens, 122
Grimms' Fairy Tales, 90
gum-tsoy, 126

Hamlet, 18, 48, 62
hawk-moths, 76, 114
hawks, 84
hayfever, 168
headache, 40, 42, 100, 178
heart ailments, 154
heart attacks, 28
Helena, 152
helenin, 152
hemorrhoids, 194
Henry V, 18
Henry VI, 78
Herodotus, 56
herpes, 122
heterostyly, 18, 92
Hippocrates, 146
hips, 64
honey-glands, 102
Hopi Indians, 190
Horace, 144
Huilliche Indians, 32
hummingbirds, 44, 114, 160
hunting potion, 28
hybrid, 32, 126, 168, 172
hypericine, 108
hypotensive activity, 80
hysteria, 50, 170

I Ching, 140
Illyria, 172
inflamed eyes, 72
inflorescence, 140, 174
insecticide, 100
Insectivorous Plants, 118
insectivorous plants, 118, 176
insect repellant, 148
internal bleeding, 176
inulin, 152
ipecac, 200
iridin, 112
iris, 78, 112
iron, 36
Iroquois Indians, 54, 170
isovaleric acid, 82
itches, 72, 108, 136

James I, 148
jaundice, 108, 140

Kalm, Peter, 68, 80
kapok, 182
keel, 58, 94, 100, 138
Kellog Biological Station, 54
kidney, 40, 122, 168
kidney stones, 48, 74
King Lear, 146

labellum, 50
latex, 14, 96, 170, 200
laurel law, 68
laxative, 176, 194

leaflet, 64, 92
lettuce, 170
Linnaeus, 20, 22, 36, 68, 102,
    110, 120, 140, 142, 144,
    164
liver ailments, 36
lobeline, 160
loganberry, 72
Longfellow, Henry
    Wadsworth, 112
Louis VII, King, 78
love potion, 160
Lumbee Indians, 178
lupine, 104

Mae Wests, 182
magnoflorine, 48
Malecite Indians, 124
mandrake root, 30
Mapuche Indians, 30
Margaret of Anjou, 102
Medea, 130
Menelaus, 152
Menominee Indians, 54, 124,
    154, 156, 176, 188, 200
Menthe, 172
menthol, 172
Meskwaki, 30, 72, 160
Micmac Indians, 12
A Midsummer Night's Dream,
    18, 114
milkweed floss, 182
milkweeds, 154, 182
Mithradates Eupator, 198
Mohawk Indians, 42
Mohegan Indians, 176
molluscicidal, 122
monarch butterfly, 96, 168
Monarda, 156
moths, 84, 106
Mount Parnassus, 166
mouth sores, 132, 188
mucilage, 28, 56, 110, 174
mums, 102
mycorrhizae, 158

NASA, 88
national flower, 168
nausea, 188
nectar, 28, 48, 84, 96, 102,
    114, 130, 134, 140, 160
nectar guides, 76, 86, 124,
    134, 160
nervine, 108, 170
nervous disorders, 46
nettles, 194
New England Botanical Club,
    34
New York Botanical Garden,
    126
night blindness, 148